FRIEND RAISING

BUILDING A MISSIONARY SUPPORT TEAM THAT LASTS

BETTY BARNETT

YWAM PUBLISHING

P.O. BOX 55787   SEATTLE, WA 98155

YWAM Publishing is the publishing ministry of Youth With A Mission. Youth With A Mission (YWAM) is an international missionary organization of Christians from many denominations dedicated to presenting Jesus Christ to this generation. To this end, YWAM has focused its efforts in three main areas: (1) Training and equipping believers for their part in fulfilling the Great Commission (Matthew 28:19), (2) Personal evangelism, and (3) Mercy ministry (medical and relief work).

For a free catalog of books and materials, contact:

YWAM Publishing
Address: P.O. Box 55787, Seattle, WA 98155
Telephone: (425) 771-1153 or (800) 922-2143
E-mail: ywampublishing@cs.com
Web site: www.ywampublishing.com

Friend Raising
Copyright © 1991 by Betty J. Barnett
Second Edition © 2003 by Betty J. Barnett

10 09 08 07 06 05 04 03   10 9 8 7 6 5 4 3 2 1

Published by YWAM Publishing
P.O. Box 55787, Seattle, Washington 98155

Unless otherwise indicated, Scripture quotations are taken from the *Holy Bible, New International Version*, copyright © 1973, 1978, 1984 by the International Bible Society. Used by permission of Zondervan Bible Publishers.

Verses marked KJV are taken from the *King James Version* of the Bible.

Verses marked Good News are taken from *The Bible in Today's English Version* (Good News Bible), © American Bible Society 1966, 1971, 1976. Used by permission.

Library of Congress Cataloging-in-Publication Data
Barnett, Betty J. (Betty Jean), 1953–
   Friend raising : building a missionary support team that lasts / Betty
J. Barnett.— Rev. ed.
      p. cm.
   ISBN 1-57658-283-3
   1. Missions—Finance. I. Title.
   BV2081.B37 2003
   266'.0068'1—dc21   2002156453

ISBN 1-57658-283-3

Printed in the United States of America.

CONTENTS

FOREWORD

BETTY BARNETT EXUDES JOY. SHE HAS BEEN PART OF YOUTH With A Mission for more than fifteen years, primarily working on the same YWAM campus as my family. I have watched her consistently practice the loving Christian friendship she teaches.

Betty speaks publicly on behalf of the work of YWAM. We trust her because we know her. She is a leader and influences many of our staff and students.

Betty has lived out this book. She speaks from faithful experience. Her teaching is not only practical but scriptural. Because it's scriptural, it will work in every part of the world, in all cultures.

Teaching on this subject is vastly needed among missionaries and other Christians determined to see Christ's last command fulfilled. As you walk through the pages of this book, a subject often avoided because of fear or confusion will be enlightened by Scripture.

The Lord often spoke of money. The Bible mentions it thousands of times. As Christians we need to recognize that money is an integral part of our lives and of the ministry. As we do what God has called us to do, we will have to walk in faith with regard to money. We will also have to walk in spiritual warfare, for it is an area in which our enemy has had undue influence.

The Lord has so ordained it that we will not walk alone in either faith or warfare. We walk together with friends to accomplish His will. This book will help you learn the dynamic of godly friendship in fulfilling all Jesus Christ has given us to do.

LOREN CUNNINGHAM
Founder, Youth With A Mission

I am carried
on the shoulders of those
who cannot see the
landscape I describe.
I owe them
far more than my weight.

A WORD FROM
THE AUTHOR

IN THE TEN YEARS SINCE THE FIRST EDITION OF THIS BOOK was written, the principles it describes have not changed. If anything, they have become more indelibly imprinted by God upon my heart and in my life. However, some information and forms of communication have changed significantly with time and technology, and it is therefore time for an update.

For many years I have presented much of the following material to Christians on both sides of the missionary fence: to the missionaries themselves and to the supporters of those missionaries. The response has been overwhelmingly positive. Thus, with continued commitment to the Great Commission and the Greatest Commandment, I pray that you, too, will be nurtured through these principles and that this book will help equip you for all God is calling you to!

At God's prompting, in order to stay true to the purpose of this book, I do not benefit financially from the sales of *Friend Raising* but set aside all author proceeds to help release others into missions. Just as generosity is a primary theme of *Friend Raising*, generosity occurred dramatically throughout the book's production. Many others involved in the preparation of the first edition gave generously, receiving no financial compensation.

My grateful acknowledgement first goes to Mary Somers, my diligent assistant at the time, who spent countless hours and days "chained" to a transcribing machine, transforming my lectures on tape into written pages (her own story begins in chapter 9). She then laboriously snatched elements of each, compiling them into coherent segments. My dear friend Judith Dupree graciously gave editorial advice, as well as her own pieces of "word art," the fresh descriptions of friendship that have been beautifully embellished by the gift of Suzanne Messing's calligraphy. My committed editor, Jimi Miller, gave numerous hours and days of gentle but firm word surgery and reconstruction, cutting, squeezing, etc. My nephew Mark Barnett, an aspiring writer, gave me encouraging feedback after being one of the first readers of the nearly finished manuscript. Dr. Carl Armerding has provided much-appreciated encouragement and feedback, especially with several critical theological issues. Several others also contributed to making this book more complete: Tom Boyle and Sandi Tompkins gave significant final editing suggestions, Barbara Overgaard developed the study questions on pages 169–173, and Gary Summers created the Friendship Record on pages 185–186. I must also acknowledge my supporters, some of whom have faithfully supported me for over twenty years. They have been the ones through whom God has taught me the most. To these and many others, I am grateful. All of us involved gave freely, believing that our labor of love would not go without effect.

I do not always live up to all that is within this book, but I am committed to God's principles. He continues to teach me and lead me, even as I periodically stumble. (My supporters can vouch for my failures as well as successes.)

This presentation is by no means exhaustive on the subject of support raising. Other highly useful materials are available, some of which are mentioned in the "Where to Go for More Help" section beginning on page 175.

My heart aches for the many who do not participate in missions because of the fear of support raising. I grieve over those who, after having responded to God's call to missionary service, have struggled unsuccessfully to raise and maintain adequate support, then have dropped out altogether. This book is dedicated to those willing laborers who have faltered in their hopes of raising support. My prayer is that these principles will instill renewed hope and be used by God to equip many to walk worthy of our calling, empowered by our Lord Jesus Christ, confident in His provision.

Help!

The three-and-a-half-hour flight from Los Angeles to Minneapolis crept by slowly. Every minute seemed to produce a new anxiety. I was going home to ask people to support my new ministry financially.

As we were about to land, I wiped the sweat from my clammy palm. The man across the aisle from me was reading *Death of a Salesman*. "How appropriate," I thought. I felt like a salesman. And I thought I was going to die.

—Bonnie C. Bishop, "Asking for Money,"
World Christian Magazine, 1986, Nov./Dec., p. 28.

— 1

THE DILEMMA OF RAISING SUPPORT

MANY CHRISTIANS CONSIDERING FULL-TIME MISSIONARY service are more fearful of support raising than of being martyred on the mission field. If you stand on that side of the fence, you are not alone. However, thousands of full-timers stand securely on the other side of the fence, proving God's faithfulness over and over.

Having lived without a predictable paycheck for more than twenty years, I personally would need a special directive from God to turn from this way of life. In spite of the challenges, I am convinced that it is a privileged lifestyle. God has faithfully met my needs while revealing to me His principles for support raising. These principles can be summarized as intimacy in relationships, interdependence, mutual love and sharing, and bearing one another's burdens. I could easily have missed many facets of God's unsearchable ways had I been simply receiving a predictable amount of money each month in a missionary paycheck all these years.

The Revolution: Independence vs. Interdependence

Contemporary cultures breed independence and self-suffi-ciency. We've been well trained by such phrases as, "Make your own way in this world!" "Don't be lazy!" "You can do it!"

Both history and personal experience prove, however, that we are ill equipped to make it on our own. Satan's lie that we are indeed able separates us from one another and from God, whose Word neither says nor implies that "God helps those who help themselves." In fact, "No man is an island," as history often shows.

Aspiring to independence from God caused Satan's fall from heaven. Grasping for independence subsequently destroyed relationships in the Garden of Eden (Gen. 3) and continues throughout history at the heart of all separation from God and from others.

Most of us are programmed with cultural how-to's that say, "Don't lean on anyone. The self-made man is the one admired." Many potential missionaries are tempted to say, "I can't ask for money. I'd be embarrassed. I don't know how to accept. Can't I just have a part-time job on the side?"

Such statements, which in one sense challenge us to responsibility, also spawn a death-producing independence contrary to the kingdom of God. This independence is rooted in pride, whereas interdependence is rooted in humility. God's Word reveals to us our weaknesses as mere humans while at the same time offering us a personal, intimate rela-tionship with our awesome, powerful God. Only through relationship with Him and with one another do we become strong. Only through humility are we free to acknowledge our need for God and others.

Ironically, the more we try to be strong without the help of others, the more we are weakened. At the same time, con-fessing our weaknesses and admitting our need for God and others strengthens us. "For when I am weak, then I am strong" (2 Cor. 12:10). Many people throughout history have failed because of their strengths rather than their weaknesses. Strengths give us a false sense of security. Two significant biblical examples are King David's adultery and subsequent murder of Uriah (2 Sam. 11) and Peter's denial that he would ever disown Jesus (Mark 14). Our strength comes when we humbly cry out, "Now to him who is able to do immeasurably more than all we ask or imagine..." (Eph. 3:20).

Christ came to establish the principles of the kingdom of God on earth, principles designed to restore relationships broken by independence and pride. We, therefore, must consciously reject independence in our own lives and conscientiously cultivate interdependence with one another and with God. Only then can we, as missionaries, not only model interdependence but also teach it to others.

Recognizing and understanding the vast difference between interdependence and the avoidance of responsibility is vitally important. It's a question of motive. Interdependence does not avoid responsibility but rather assigns it to diversified activities. It's not a matter of self-preservation but of preserving and furthering a mutual work. For instance, I am responsible not only for *my* work but also for *ours!*

The call to a faith-support lifestyle is a call to interdependence. In today's culture this is revolutionary!

Missionaries for the Lord are not sparring verbally with others to get their money. Interdependence is not Christian welfare. It is the joining of forces to defend the faith and to fight the good fight.

"Though one may be overpowered, two can defend themselves. A cord of three strands is not quickly broken" (Eccles. 4:12).

Firm Foundations: God's Master Plan in Creation

One day in Hawaii, as I stood atop a cliff overlooking the Pacific, violent winds whipped across the whitecapped sea and roared up the cliff, driving me back to a grove of old trees. The broad tree trunks hardly quivered, even as the top branches flailed wildly. The calm, protective haven contrasted starkly with the windswept sea.

Safely surrounded by the ancient trees, I saw that nature itself was demonstrating to me God's principle of interdependence in the area of missionary support. I sensed the Lord saying, "The tree's strength depends on its broad network of roots. Your strength depends on the wide network of interdependent people with you in My service. Therefore, in the battle you are able to withstand the fiery darts of the enemy."

I understood that had the trees in the wind been brittle and alone or had shallow roots, they could easily have been uprooted and hurled away.

My attention was also drawn to a bouncing five-spoked spider web. Its creator had designed and maintained it to withstand the force of the gale. As I watched the web dance in the wind, the spider meticulously reinforced spoke after spoke. I understood that we must constantly reinforce the spokes in our missionary network. Not only must we have a number of "spokes" in our missionary framework, we also must constantly reinforce our "netting"—our network. None of us can go it alone. If we try to do so, our lives will become like broken trees or torn spider webs.

Setting the Stage

In preparation for both short- and long-term mission service, personal conviction about support raising will make or break our ability to realize ministry income: Is it fundamentally right? Is it good? Is it holy? Am I worthy of support?

Did you know that Jesus had financial supporters? Luke 8:3 tells that "Joanna…Susanna; and many others…were helping to support them [Jesus and the twelve disciples] out of their own means." The apostle Paul himself wrote, "…the Lord has commanded that those who preach the gospel should receive their living from the gospel" (1 Cor. 9:14). Elijah, while living in a ravine, was fed for a time by ravens, until God sent him to a widow in Zarephath to ask for support (1 Kings 17). His silence and his soliciting were both in obedience to God.[1]

If raising support proves too great a burden, prospective long-term workers without firm support bases often become short-term workers. Identifying the causes of inadequate support and discovering the keys to God's remedies in His Word can bring a turnabout from fatigue, frustration, and failure.

In short, conviction and attitude permeate everything we do in life—ministry, evangelism, and missions per se—and often open or close the door to God's storehouse of provisions for our missionary support.

Confirming Your Call

One of the first things to be tested in your friend-raising vs. fund-raising venture is your "call."

Is the call of God stronger than the call of the world? What is your anchor in the midst of calm or stormy winds and crashing waves?

"Listen to me, you who pursue righteousness and who seek the LORD: Look to the rock from which you were cut and to the quarry from which you were hewn" (Isa. 51:1).

Has God called? Have you been summoned by the living God to become a missionary and to embrace a lifestyle of trust to the extreme of no guaranteed paycheck? If in fact you have been called by Him, then you *are* worthy. He has declared you so.

Even though confidence may waver from time to time, deep down you know if God has called you. I remember numerous occasions when I have sensed with crystal clarity God's calling on my life. I have experienced tingles of excitement as well as that deep "...peace of God, which transcends all understanding..." (Phil. 4:7) as the Lord has opened new chapters in my life.

Feelings, however, can also lead to roller-coaster rides causing doubt and loss of confidence, but the fact of God's calling does not waver. What did He say? How was it confirmed? We often need friends to help us remember, to pray with us in our uncertainty, to encourage us in our doubt. We personally need to go back to basics and dig for the truth we once held firmly.

"Being confident of this, that he who began a good work in you will carry it on to completion until the day of Christ Jesus" (Phil. 1:6).

The security of our calling will be frequently tested. Lack of confidence in what God has said will greatly affect our communication with others, who will not want to support a missionary with an uncertain calling. Hang on to your Rock; remain securely anchored in Him and in what He has spoken to you. You know what He said. Walk accordingly.

Sharing with Others

The most important people to contact first regarding your call are those who have a position of authority in your life and those who will be significantly affected by your decision regarding missionary service. This includes parents, other family members, and your pastor. Including these key people in your decision-making process is critical. Proverbs 15:22 warns us, "Plans fail for lack of counsel, but with many advisers they succeed."

An act of "honoring your father and mother" is consulting them on major life decisions, such as a missionary career. Respecting them by asking their opinion is important to them and to us. However, we may be misunderstood. Mark 6:4 applies not only to prophets but also to where *we* are most likely to be misunderstood: "Only in his hometown, among his relatives and in his own house is a prophet without honor." Those closest to us often have great insight about our strengths and weaknesses as well as limited awareness of our potential. It's often difficult for them to see us in a new light, with the potential the Lord sees. We may have to respond with, "We must obey God rather than men!" like Peter and the apostles (Acts 5:29).

Once I was lecturing in Japan on friend raising. Afterward a young man commented, "I submitted to my pastor. I went to him and said, 'I believe God's calling me to work with college students in Japan, and I believe I'm to go soon. Would the church support me? Would you be behind me? Would you pray about it?' The pastor said, 'I'll pray about it.'"

Later the pastor met with the young man and said, "I met with the missions committee, and we believe you should have four years of Bible college before going to the mission field. Then we will support you fully." The young man responded, "OK, I'll pray about it and get back to you." Both sides responded well to each other in the face of obvious disagreement.

The young man went back to the Lord. "What do I do? Was I wrong? Are they wrong? Are they right?" The Lord answered, "I called you to work with college students now because *you* are now of college age. This is the time for you to go."

The youth returned to the pastor with a submissive attitude and said, "I'm sorry. I believe God's telling me to go now." The pastor said, "Fine," implying no support.

This young man needed to obey the Lord rather than man when there was an obvious difference of opinion. Submission to God always means obedience. Submission to others does not always mean obedience to their desires or understanding. We are to take what the pastor says very seriously, *but* it isn't the final word. At the same time, we need to have a submissive response toward our spiritual authorities.

This young man could have blurted, "I'm sorry, but I'm going to do it because God told me to. You guys are wrong!" That would not have been an act of submission. Instead he retained and respected the relationship, even though there was obvious disagreement about what God was saying. If he continues to communicate with his church leadership, not breaking the relationships over the disagreement on timing, I believe they will be part of his long-term support team, whether it includes finances or not.

We are to continue to love and respect our spiritual authorities, submitting to them, even from afar.

In another instance, a friend of mine who was preparing to depart for the mission field was told by his pastor and elders that they disagreed with the timing of his planned departure. They felt that he should stay home and continue to establish himself in their church while beginning a youth ministry in their community, similar to what he desired to start in a Latin country with street kids. They believed this would be an important foundation-laying time for him in future ministry. Even though it was difficult for him to accept the change in plans, he felt the Lord wanted him to follow his spiritual leaders' counsel. He remained in his home community and served well, preparing for long-term ministry after a season of learning and maturing. By submission to his pastor and elders, he was benefiting from their wisdom and concern for his long-term success.

Another young missionary from Papua New Guinea told me that he was directed by his church leadership to go to a Bible theological college for three years. They promised to support him and pay for all his college fees. However, Robert felt strongly that he was to join Youth With A Mission (YWAM) and attend the introductory program, Discipleship Training School (DTS). His church disagreed with his decision and said they would not support him.

During the six months of the DTS, Robert wrote to his church monthly, though he didn't hear back from them. He shared how and what he was doing. After the DTS was completed, he returned to his home church and shared his experiences and what God had done. "They saw a change in me...and from that time on, my pastor was interested in me. I told him that my vision was to work with YWAM at the Honolulu base...and he was excited about it. He was also interested in sending other young people to the DTS."

When Robert returned to the Honolulu YWAM base to continue in missionary studies, his church paid for his airfare, approximately $1,300. Robert feels called to missions long-term. He regularly corresponds with leaders in his church. "We write to each other now. We have a lot of close relationships....They are like parents to me now. I've preached in the church. They commissioned me....We had a tremendous time."

I'm aware of other situations where the pastor and missions committee spoke for God as they encouraged the person to delay his or her departure for the mission field. They recommended getting more foundation and having greater involvement in the church, while growing in maturity. They recognized that weaknesses in these areas could cause potential disaster in the pressure cooker of the mission field.

Either way, we need to be submissive and honoring. "Young men, in the same way be submissive to those who are older. All of you, clothe yourselves with humility toward one another, because 'God opposes the proud but gives grace to the humble'" (1 Pet. 5:5).

Pillars of Strength

We're building the house of God. As with all structures, strong support is required for long-term durability through storms and harsh seasons. As His living stones and builders, we need scriptural undergirding for our pillars to "hold up the roof."

"If the Lord does not build the house, the work of the builders is useless…" (Ps. 127:1, Good News).

Four pillars are needed: friend raising, generosity, communication, and prayer with promises. They ensure protection and covering so we can venture into the Enemy's territory for battle. The first pillar, friend raising, causes us to evaluate our priorities. Will we "take the money and run"? Or is there a higher way?

Note

1. For further biblical study on God's ways of financially supporting workers in the temple or the church, see the following passages: Exod. 25:1–2, 35:4–5; Num. 8:14, 18:21–24; Deut. 14:27, 16:17; 1 Sam. 9:7–8; Neh. 2:1–8, 13:14; Matt. 10:5–15, Luke 10:1–8, 22:35–38; Acts 10:2–5, 20:32–35; Rom. 15:20–24; 2 Cor. 1:16; 2 Cor. 8–9. 12:13–19; Gal. 6:6; 1 Thess. 2:9; 2 Thess. 3:7–10; 1 Tim. 5:17–18, 6:17–19; 3 John 5–8.

—

Friendship is a place to hide in,
to abide in —
not to escape the world,
but to face it well.

—

- 2

THE FIRST PILLAR: FRIEND RAISING

USING THE TERM "FRIEND RAISING" RATHER THAN "FUND-raising" captures the essence of support raising. It broadens its meaning and promotes the richness in relationships that God wants us to build.

We are to seek first the kingdom of God, not the dollar. We are to care more for people as friends than for their potential contributions to our ministry.

The kingdom of God, made up of followers and servants of the King, focuses us away from the world's value system toward a godly development of friendships. Our needs are met as a by-product, not as the goal.

When money is our primary aim, everything we do in support raising is tainted with the love of money. When friendship is our primary motive, we aim for the heart of God and His ultimate fulfillment for us: love for Him and love for one another, the object of the two great commandments.

Lifestyle of Exchange

We are called to a lifestyle of exchange—of giving and receiving. The Lord's business is raising our resources; we are to build relationships as He leads. By seeking to serve our friends, we give them opportunities to share in our lives and ministries. Others can tell whether our motives are to cherish and enjoy them or to use them to serve our own goals.

Barb Mossberg, a long-term YWAM missionary in the remote mountain tribal village of Bontoc, Philippines, is a fine example of a friend raiser. When I saw her in the late 1980s, she mentioned, "I'm receiving approximately $700 monthly in unsolicited support." I exclaimed, "Barb, tell me what you're doing—you *must* be doing something right!" She described what I call a "poured out" lifestyle toward her friends and family. Each week she spent approximately eighteen hours writing letters and sending photographs back home, encouraging friends and reporting ministry results.

Barb says, "I love people and value my friendships. I fear that with my being so far away, they will forget me. I write to keep them writing back and because I want them praying for me and the ministry. That's more important than getting money from them. I ask how their families are and what prayer concerns they have. I tell them about this country and give eyewitness stories about the people with whom I work. I also describe my hands-on ministry, hoping many will become interested in missions."

Barb has a personal prayer commitment to see one hundred young people from her hometown in Minnesota go into mission work as a result of her prayers and encouragement. Soon after I had seen Barb, I was sharing this story with a group of missionaries-in-training. Two of them piped up, "We're here because of Barb Mossberg! We're two of eight we know of so far this year who have gone into missions because of her." I was deeply moved.

Just before Barb first left Minnesota for the Philippines, a farmer gave her ten pounds of his leftover vegetable seeds for the Filipino villagers. Later Barb sent photographs back to the farmer showing the abundant results of his generosity. Consequently he encouraged other farmers in his Sunday-school class to send Barb their extra seeds, and they sent her one hundred pounds. Barb distributed the seeds among five different villages, which began producing an abundance of vegetables for their communities.

Another man in Barb's home church sent her a check for $250 to use as she saw fit. Barb prayed, then built pigpens and invested the $250 in four baby pigs. Only God could inspire such an idea! She wrote the man a letter, enclosing photographs. Her letter described the results of his $250 investment in pigs, which would later generate income for a scholarship fund for Filipino missionary trainees.

Through these acts Barb knit her hometown family and friends in Minnesota with her new family and friends in the Philippines. They would otherwise never have made contact. Both givers and receivers were blessed, and the kingdom of God was expanded.

At one point Barb was receiving so much financial support that she asked her supporters if she could designate some of the money for Filipino missionaries who had little or no support. Permission was granted. Those Filipinos then began writing to the people in Barb's church, sharing their own stories from the mission field. Generosity in Minnesota birthed generosity in the Philippines, which in turn birthed missionaries for God's kingdom.

A few years after I saw Barb, she wrote me a note that she was no longer spending eighteen hours a week writing letters (whew!). She wrote, "At this time, I'm spending about eight to ten hours per week in communication with friends." Yet, she commented, "The support remains at about $700 per month, and I still do not have to ask for a nickel of it. I often get gifts from friends and relatives who are not even Christians, because they care about me and like hearing from me."

Friend raising means loving and caring for others so that they and the kingdom of God will be built up at the same time.

Intimacy: Our Deepest Need

Mother Teresa was often asked what she believed causes the greatest suffering. Her response? "Loneliness." From one who was continually confronted by starvation, disease, and death, the answer is surprising. Yet it's not surprising to God.

God created Adam for friendship. Then He saw that Adam needed friendship and intimacy not only with Him but also with another human being. Intimacy is the foundation of our lives. We were designed for it, and it is only there that our deepest desires are fulfilled.

"Friendship is rare on earth," wrote Oswald Chambers. "It means identity in thought and heart and spirit."[1]

The world, with its religion of materialism, substitutes worldly riches for those of the kingdom. But satisfaction does not come through the riches of this world. They entice but never deliver. They appeal to the flesh, but the need is in the soul.

In his book *The Friendship Factor* Dr. Alan Loy McGinnis observes, "If we build more windows and fewer walls, we will have more friends." He also describes openness with others as a key to mental and emotional health. Dr. McGinnis describes a conversation he had with a potential client who was reeling from a divorce: "Are you close to anybody? ...Is there someone you can tell everything to?" She replied, "Oh yes,...we tell each other all our secrets. We're life-friends." At the end of the hour session, he agreed with her that "as long as she had a confidante, she didn't need a shrink."[2]

In our fragmented society of broken families and broken relationships, our greatest ache comes from loneliness. Where there's a void of friends, there's a desperate, crying need for intimacy. As a result, many search for intimacy in the wrong places and with the wrong motives. There are inherent dangers in mistaking the short-run benefits of financial support for the eternal blessings of intimacy.

Two of my own experiences give good examples of how God changed my heart's motivation from the love of money to a far greater love.

While I was on staff at the U.S. Center for World Mission, I found myself nurturing a relationship with a well-off couple—I'll call them Jerry and Bernadette—who supported me. I honestly appreciated them for their faithfulness, but initially I had looked at them with dollar signs in my eyes.

Soon after my dad died of cancer (I'll talk more about that later), Bernadette also was battling cancer, and I could see that she was dying. Many people did not know how to respond to her or what to say. They felt awkward in the face of impending death. But I had just walked through it with my dad, and since we'd been friends for a while, Jerry and Bernadette allowed me into their lives.

Knowing how important it is for someone to stay with a terminally ill loved one, I sat on Bernadette's bed one day while Jerry went to the pharmacy. I wanted to let Bernadette talk about the cancer, to be real and transparent.

I wanted to say, "Let's not super-spiritualize and ignore the pain and ugliness."

Because of her cancer's similarities with Dad's, she was able to tell me of her own physical "uglies." She knew she was dying, yet she had a striking peace "that passes understanding." She knew she was on her way to heaven.

She and I cried together. Our hearts were touched with pain. We weren't dishonoring the Lord by experiencing the pain. We were honestly touching "the good, the bad, and the ugly."

Jerry returned from his errand. He asked, "So, Betty, do you need any money?"

His question threw me off guard, and I felt like screaming out, "Don't bring money into this bedroom! I just lost my dad; your wife is dying! Who cares about money? My heart aches for *you* and Bernadette and the struggles you're going through."

Then I realized the change that had taken place in my heart. I thought, *Thank you, God, that there's been such a switch in my mind-set. I don't care whether they support me or not. I just want to love them.*

I finally stammered, "No, I don't think so. I think I'm okay." I truly didn't know at that moment if I needed money. It wasn't uppermost in my thoughts. Love relationships were.

I later sent them anthuriums, brilliant red tropical flowers from Hawaii. I wanted to brighten their day. I hesitated at first. *They'll think I've got too much support. Perhaps I shouldn't send them.* Then I thought, *Who cares? I love them. That's what matters. They're hurting, and I want to soften the pain.*

They were thrilled with the flowers. Their daughter decorated the house with them. Their home was brightened with patches of red anthuriums because of a simple act of love in a time of painful need.

Two days before I left on a trip to Asia in July of that year, I received a phone call from Jerry. "Bernadette and I just put a $200 check in the mail for your trip—not for necessities. Treat yourself! If you get stuck and need a plane ticket, you're free to use it, but we'd prefer that you use it on yourself."

I was touched by this sign of their love, especially because, for the first time, I heard it in his voice that his wife was dying.

Bernadette died the day I left for Asia.

I received the news while I was in the Philippines. I immediately took a long walk, and the tears welled up in my eyes. I'd grown to love them deeply. Her death hurt, even though I knew she had been ushered into the presence of her Lord and King, Jesus Christ. As I shed my tears, I understood the deep work God had done in our relationship and especially in my heart: the dollar signs in my eyes were long gone.

A second experience, one that related to my family, also demonstrated the deep change within me.

Greg, my oldest half-brother, came to me and said, "Betty, we [the rest of the family] want to give you a $5,000 gift for taking care of Dad before he died. We appreciate what you did in keeping him out of the hospital and caring for him at home."

My initial response was, "Please don't turn what was a labor of love into 'a work for hire.' I took care of Dad because I loved him, not because I expected to get paid. I don't want the $5,000."

Greg responded, "I understand. But regardless of what you do with the money, we want to give it to you."

After I considered the circumstances, I realized it was all right to accept the money. The rest of the family had been unable to take care of Dad in the same way I had. As a result they felt an imbalance that needed to be made right. This gift was their way of handling it. To refuse would have perpetuated the imbalance.

I've since reflected on that interchange, realizing that the deep work of the Lord in my life was demonstrated by my uncharacteristic hesitancy to take the money.

Can we look $5,000, or any amount of money, in the face and say, "If this isn't right, I don't want it"? Such a possibility only comes through the Lord. It reflects a supernatural work by the Holy Spirit of freeing our hearts from the love of money!

Spontaneous Intimacy

On one plane trip, I met a woman and her nine-year-old son. He had brain cancer, and they were going to a doctor in San Diego as a last-ditch effort. I understood some of her feelings.

I shared how my dad had recently died of cancer and asked, "Isn't it amazing how your values change at a time like this?"

She answered, "Absolutely! A month ago, I lost a diamond earring. My husband observed that a year ago I would have been terribly upset. But now it's not even important."

How true! Of what value are diamonds, bank accounts, or houses when we are about to lose our loved one?

It boils down to relationships. This woman and I had been stripped down to God-designed values: our love for family and friends. Satan has tainted our lives so that the things of this world have become idols. But when death is imminent, who cares about money?

Only when we share deep needs, joys, and disappointments does intimacy occur and friendship deepen. The levels of intimacy will vary among our supporters and friends. A few will share deep secrets with us—and we with them. We trust each other with potentially wounding information about ourselves. More often than not, we are on the listening end.

Listening, the Gateway to Friendship

"He who answers before listening—that is his folly and his shame" (Prov. 18:13).

Listening is one of the greatest dynamics in friendship. When we pull out the latest "ooh, aah" mission stories to impress friends, we are not listening. When we tell our exciting stories without an attitude of humility, it alienates others.

"If I have the gift of prophecy and can fathom all mysteries and all knowledge, and if I have a faith that can move mountains, but have not love, I am nothing" (1 Cor. 13:2).

Knowledge without humility breeds alienation.

On the other hand, sharing the "word of our testimony" with humility woos others toward the kingdom of God and ministers life. It becomes a transfer of life instead of simply a transfer of truth.

Our approach in evangelism is similar. We can see people not as persons but as targets that need saving. But nobody is fooled. They know it, we know it, and God knows it. It's the pursuit of a goal—a point of conquering—not an act of love.

Those of us in full-time Christian service, especially overseas service, carry back home with us language and customs different from those of our own culture. This makes it difficult at times for many of our longtime friends to understand and relate to us. A "Barb Mossberg lifestyle" of regular communication with people back home can significantly ease this difficulty, as long as we continue to emphasize the friendship aspect of our relationships.

During visits back home, our primary role should be to listen. Too often we are quick to speak of our ministry, quick to validate what we are doing out on the mission field and what we think, and we are seldom quick to listen.

Those who support us have needs too. No doubt many will ask questions, but often their primary need is to talk with someone they respect and trust. Because we are in missionary service, they often have a high expectation of our spirituality (whether we deserve it or not). They are often looking for a sounding board and godly counsel. I learned this the hard way.

One summer after some intense recruiting for YWAM, I visited friends in California. I flew in from Texas and had twenty-four hours before my flight home to Hawaii. I took the airport bus to visit a special friend who lived with two other friends of mine. I hadn't seen any of them for over a year.

When I arrived, they were playing cards. One of them said, "Sit down, Betty. We'll just be a few more minutes."

I sat for forty-five minutes, three feet away from them as they went on with the card game—no conversation, just cards being passed back and forth across the table.

I began thinking, *Is this any way to treat a guest?*

Later, my special friend, who had been one of the card players, drove me to the house where I would be staying. I said to him, "That really stunk." (Because of our good friendship, I could make such statements!) "That was no way to treat anyone, whether they know me or not. We've been friends. We used to go to church together. Why did they treat me that way?"

He answered, "Betty, let me give you their side of the story. Yes, I admit the hospitality was lousy. But, well, we don't understand you anymore. You speak a language we don't speak. You live a life we don't live. It's hard to relate to you."

I was shocked but pierced by the truth. I had become more a "living brochure" than a friend, intent on inspiring my friends with mission stories. I wanted to impress them with stunning events in the kingdom of God, trying to get them involved in missions. It created a chasm between us. I was treating them as targets, not as friends!

I felt God gently say, "Betty, be quiet. Learn to listen."

That lesson in listening paid off dramatically when I spent time with another friend, a single Christian woman with a deep prayer life. This time I listened.

As she shared the events and struggles in her life, I listened and simply asked nonthreatening questions. When she told me about her counseling sessions with a therapist, I asked her if she thought she was getting godly counsel.

She said, "Yes, I believe I am." She then surprised me with the news that she had had sex with a guy five months earlier.

I said, "Wow! How did you handle that?"

Her therapist, she said, had condoned her actions, explaining that her experience was an affirming one, helping her to more fully accept herself.

I asked, "Did you challenge him with what the Bible says?"

She said she had confronted him with scriptures on sexual immorality, yet he still believed that what she had done was good for her. He so influenced her that she went out and bought contraceptives.

After about three hours of listening and asking questions, I finally felt the freedom to speak "a word in season." I told her that I didn't believe she was getting godly counsel. I did believe she had two options: either pray about terminating the therapy sessions or ask someone godly and trustworthy— her pastor, for instance—to screen everything her therapist told her, so she could test his counsel by God's Word.

My words stunned her. She had so lost her objectivity that she trusted her therapist's counsel. She eventually terminated the sessions and turned to a godly counselor. How grateful I was for God's prompting me to listen and not react to her confession with a judgmental, "You did *what?*"

Effective listening involves focusing on what is being said, above what we want to say, and refraining from interrupting, which breaks the flow of thought and sometimes halts the conversation.

Few people today are equipped to listen. We tend to offer responses with quick-fix Scripture references, coupled with simplistic do's and don'ts. We want to create instant change in someone, when God would have us listen, be a friend, and wait to offer a word from Him.

Listening takes eyes and heart as well as ears. Listen for what is *not* spoken. We must set our minds on confirming, encouraging, giving spiritual input, and also speaking the truth in love, offering correction when appropriate and when the time is right.

Listening also includes the important skill of asking questions. "A person's thoughts are like water in a deep well, but someone with insight can draw them out" (Prov. 20:5, Good News). Asking the right questions at the right time can lead to deeper relationships and more meaningful communication. Communicating genuine interest and acceptance is also essential. Effective communication includes both telling and asking, allowing others to know we have something to learn and receive from them.

Confronting

Confronting is another important dynamic of friendship: "...you who are spiritual should restore him gently. But watch yourself, or you also may be tempted" (Gal. 6:1). Once we've listened, we're able to offer a response. Be willing to speak the truth in love—*after* listening! It's a privilege that should be handled carefully, with humility. At the same time we must give our friends the opportunity to speak into our lives. We need each other!

Properly done, confronting addresses the problem in an atmosphere of love and respect, giving the person the choice of changing or not. Above all, confronting involves love and affirmation. The one confronted must not doubt that we have his or her best interests in mind. Without much prior prayer, this is an almost impossible task.

Each of us needs to pray for firsthand understanding of God's principles: "...the speech of the upright rescues them....The tongue of the righteous is choice silver....The lips of the righteous nourish many....The lips of the right-eous know what is fitting....A wicked messenger falls into trouble, but a trustworthy envoy brings healing" (Prov. 12:6; 10:20–21, 32; 13:17). May we be trustworthy envoys of the Lord, speaking only gems of encouragement and life.

Our first pillar, friend raising, is built on a lifestyle of caring for people more as friends than as sources of funding. We develop these friendships through a lifestyle of exchange, intimacy, and caring through listening. The second pillar, generosity, gives even more practical ways through which we see the kingdom of God expanded.

Notes

1. Oswald Chambers, My Utmost for His Highest (Uhrichsville, Ohio: Barbour Publishing, 1987), p. 7.
2. Alan Loy McGinnis, The Friendship Factor: How to Get Closer to the People You Care For (Minneapolis: Augsburg Publishing, 1979), pp. 10, 30.

—

When we walk with God
we are not forced
to act in a loving way.
We are compelled to.

—

THE SECOND PILLAR: GENEROSITY

DURING THE SUMMER OF 1986 I WORKED WITH A YOUTH With A Mission team passing out Bibles door to door in Mexico City. I was asked to teach on support raising to a group of missionary trainees from Guatemala—the first group of people I would teach who were from a country with very limited financial resources. Yet I believed that if God's principles were true, then they were true worldwide, in all societies, among all peoples, in all economic situations. In Mexico City, I was faced with the test of my convictions.

The day before I was to teach, I prayed, "God, what is the key to support raising that applies to all people?" A word came immediately into my mind: generosity!

Suddenly I understood—it was not others' generosity toward us but our generosity toward others that was the key. Generosity. I pondered the word and gained new understanding of the principle behind support raising. An attitude of generosity purifies our motives, keeping us wanting to serve others, not wanting to be served. With this motivation, our hearts are right before the Lord and before others, without hidden agendas of manipulation or greed.

Generosity in us breeds generosity in others. It permeates Scripture, reflecting the heart of God. "A generous man will prosper; he who refreshes others will himself be refreshed" (Prov. 11:25). We cannot prosper in ministry with pinched hearts. Whether we come from difficult backgrounds or not, we are to be generous as an example for people to see the kingdom of God in action. Generosity breaks cultural bondages that hinder giving and receiving.

The next day I shared this insight with the Guatemalans through my interpreter. When I told them about some Christians in Myanmar (formerly Burma) who set aside a handful of rice each day for their missionaries, they listened intently. I saw a spark of hope in their eyes.

I told them of a South American pastor who, while in prayer, was corrected by the Lord, "You're not teaching My whole truth to the people."

He was surprised. "What do You mean?" he asked the Lord. "We're seeing tremendous spiritual growth in our congregation!"

The Lord answered, "You're not teaching on giving and generosity."

Before he could object that his congregation was too poor to give, another revelation came into his mind: "My truth is truth, and My principles apply regardless of circumstances. Teach them."

The pastor obeyed. He began teaching on generosity, on giving, and on missions. He told them to set aside a handful of rice, a part of their fruits and vegetables, or whatever they had. He challenged them out of their extreme poverty to set aside something for the Lord. They began, and the pastor watched.

The more he taught on giving and generosity, the more his congregation gave. In their poverty, some gave perhaps just a tomato or some rice. As they gave what they were able, God began to increase their resources from which to give. God's principle of generosity brought new life to these people, and the congregation grew both in their ability to give and in their material well-being.

As I finished telling this story to the Guatemalan missionary trainees, I could see new hope on their faces. They began to "rise up in faith" to break cultural bondages dictating that their churches and entire country were too poor to support missionaries.

Earl Pitts, with YWAM in Cambridge, Ontario, describes generosity in a unique way: "The Kingdom of God's system of finances is giving and receiving. The world's system is buying and selling."[1] He goes on to explain that in buying and selling, we keep our resources to ourselves and exchange with reciprocity, a measured transaction of equal value. We all engage in buying and selling—there's a time for buying and selling and a time for giving and receiving. We need to have integration. Each fulfills important purposes. We pay rent and house payments; we buy clothes and groceries. Buying and selling are parts of life, but they should not be the consuming modes of money transactions, especially among Christians.

Two laws in nature illustrate this point. The law of gravity explains why a rock falls, while the law of aerodynamics allows a bird to fly. One law does not cancel out the other. Much of what Jesus taught and exemplified challenges us to go beyond the norm, the ordinary, the traditional "law." Just as the law of gravity does not prevent a bird from flying, giving and receiving is not canceled out by buying and selling but supersedes or transcends it. It is a kingdom activity that goes far beyond the ordinary.

Giving and receiving is to be one of the primary marks of a Christian, as Paul describes in 2 Corinthians 8:7: "But just as you excel in everything—in faith, in speech, in knowledge, in complete earnestness and in your love for us—see that you also excel in this grace of giving."

How often do we consider that we are to strive toward excellence in generosity? It is to be a lifestyle, a high calling for all Christians. Unfortunately, our personal lives and the life of the church have been so influenced by the world that it's often difficult to discern God's point of view, especially when it is such a radical one. Giving and receiving—or interdependence—is countercultural. It confronts and breaks the world's system of independence.

Jesus was outraged by the buying and selling in the temple. It so contaminated the temple that Jesus called it a den of robbers! When buying and selling consumes us and becomes the priority of our lives, we've lost the sense of how God wants to knit us together. We've fallen into the sin of "the love of money." We've lost the richness of giving and receiving.

In 1987 Richard Halversen, chaplain of the U.S. Senate, included a striking comment in his March 4 newsletter, *Perspective*. The page that normally includes devotional remarks was blank except for a quotation from 1 Timothy 6:10 (KJV): "For the love of money is the root of all evil...." He signed the page, "With profound concern." Satan would lure us into independence by the exclusive system of buying and selling. He is fully aware of the spiritual riches that will be released if we give and receive.

Generosity, or giving and receiving, involves much more than transferring goods. It transforms independent individuals into a community, bound with cords that cannot be broken. The precious things that have been given to us often hold far more value than those things we have purchased. Satan robs us, often as we sit by unaware. We must pursue God's ways of interdependence through giving and receiving, rather than the worldly virtue of brash independence. When we use the world's ways, we will have the world's brokenness; when we use God's ways, we will have His healing wholeness.

Described in the second chapter of Acts, the church after Pentecost exemplifies the integration of buying/selling and giving/receiving: "Selling their possessions and goods, they gave to anyone as he had need" (Acts 2:45). We are to give of what we have. Though it may be little, we are still to be free with it.

The love of money can plague us at both extremes, in poverty or in wealth. The temptation is to grasp with greed. We who are experiencing "seasons of want" can respond with the same unbelief and treasure-clenching as did the rich young ruler. That was the young ruler's downfall (Luke 18). In contrast, however, the widow gave what little she had, and her widow's mite was given great honor (Luke 21). The Lord knows the difficulty of generosity when one has little.

The normal flow of life includes both seasons of plenty and seasons of want. Wisdom resides in Proverbs: "…give me neither poverty nor riches, but give me only my daily bread. Otherwise, I may have too much and disown you and say, 'Who is the LORD?' Or I may become poor and steal, and so dishonor the name of my God" (Prov. 30:8–9).

We need to allow God to transform our minds so that money will take its proper place. "Do not conform any longer to the pattern of this world, but be transformed by the renewing of your mind. Then you will be able to test and approve what God's will is—his good, pleasing and perfect will" (Rom. 12:2).

An Independent Sector survey reports that 70 percent of American households make donations to charities, with the average person giving 2.1 percent of his or her income. Yet those who gave the highest percentage of their money to charity were those who earned less. Households with annual incomes below $10,000 donated a whopping 5.3 percent of their income, while those with incomes over $100,000 gave only 2.2 percent. Churchgoers gave 2.3 percent while non-churchgoers gave only 1.3 percent of their income.[2] These statistics suggest that those with more money tend to have characteristics similar to those of the rich young ruler, clinging to riches.

Doesn't it seem odd that even though churchgoers give significantly more than those who don't attend church, their giving is still far below the biblical concept of tithing? George Barna, who has conducted research for hundreds of churches and parachurch ministries, as well as Fortune 500 companies and non-profit organizations, states, "Intellectually, we believe that the primary reason God has blessed us is to enjoy life and achieve personal fulfillment. There are very few believers who, without prompting, believe that we have been blessed to be a blessing to others...the average total donations to churches over the course of the year was just $500 in 1999. That was two-thirds of all of the money the typical believer donated to all churches and non-profit organizations during the year, but represents a small fraction of the income of believers. Most amazing of all was the fact that only 8 percent of all believers tithed last year [1999]. In fact, twice as many believers (16 percent) gave nothing to their church last year as gave 10 percent or more of their income."[3] We desperately need God to transform us in our own expressions of generosity so we become more like Him, the Master of generosity.

We can easily disburse a million dollars (or turn down $5,000) within God's value system, but the world says, "Do almost anything for a million dollars." God's way is to give all for the relationship, the way Jesus did.

A historic display of generosity occurred after the devastating earthquake in Armenia in the late 1980s. Television reporters commented, "This is phenomenal. There's never been an open door like this into the Soviet Union nor such generosity toward the USSR. From around the world, people are giving. Forty-six of the world's nations are responding. Most of the blood is being sent from Afghanistan. Lebanon is sending money."

Tears came to my eyes as I listened to the report. God's principles of giving and receiving, especially between arch-enemy nations, were making international news! These principles bridged a gap never crossed before—a stunning event, not only in the physical realm but also in the spiritual. One can't help wondering if this event helped precipitate the collapse of the Iron Curtain!

As missionaries in support raising, we are being invited and discipled into a lifestyle of giving and receiving. At the same time, we are confronted by the world's propaganda: "I earned this. I'm going to keep it! Earn your own!"

We can respond in one of two ways. We can be hurt and recoil with, "I'm a beggar. I want a regular paycheck like normal people. I don't want donations that make me feel like I owe people." Or we can refocus on God's principles of friendship and generosity. A feeling of indebtedness comes from the world's buying-and-selling mentality that says, "I owe them exactly what they gave me." Generosity involves freedom with no indebtedness except that of love.

The most precious donations I have received in missionary service have been from people I did not believe could afford to give anything. One family that has supported me for much of my years in ministry has lived with a tight income themselves. Yet they have generously supported my ministry. They give beyond their ability, and I see God blessing and honoring them as a result.

Paul redefined receiving gifts as a genuine privilege. We often feel guilty for receiving donations and fail to understand God's hidden agenda. To live a life of generosity, especially among the brethren, is a calling and, more importantly, a privilege from the Lord. Most of us find it much easier to give than to receive. We miss God's and others' gifts with this attitude. Any time there is *only* giving or *only* receiving between two parties, it is unhealthy. Each of us is built for both. We all need to be regularly involved in both giving and receiving as part of God's design for our healthiness. Otherwise we may become more like welfare recipients or patronizing benefactors.

There is no lack of money for God's work. The money is there, but much of it is locked into the buying-and-selling systems that have consumed and robbed the church. Our own generosity can release others from ordinary buying and selling into giving and receiving.

We impart whatever we live. Buying and selling is infectious. Giving and receiving is also infectious! We can impart generosity to others, seeing God's resources released and the kingdom of God increased. But our motives must continually be purified by the Lord. If we induce people to give by obligation, pressure, or guilt, we stifle true generosity and everyone misses the benefits. In addition, the outcome could be short-term financial results but long-term broken relationships.

Both giver and receiver are blessed through generosity. Also, balance is achieved as giving and receiving occurs: "Then there will be equality" (2 Cor. 8:14). Both parties receive satisfaction from the gift exchange, one having given out of his or her excess to help the other's shortage, yet both are blessed. To block generosity hinders both sides! Both lose. No wonder Satan robs the church of giving and receiving! When generosity is stifled, both givers and receivers are robbed not only physically but also spiritually, no longer built up as God intended.

"...They gave as much as they were able, and even beyond their ability. Entirely on their own, they urgently pleaded with us for the privilege of sharing in this service to the saints" (2 Cor. 8:3–4).

The Macedonians, even though extremely poor, understood giving as a privilege and pleaded to be able to give. They were more affected by God's ways than by their sparse means.

Times will come when we (and others!) will feel that we are so needy that we have nothing to give, nothing to be generous with. This is our greatest test! God may nudge us to give what little we have, even in extreme poverty. Like the impoverished Macedonians and the widow who gave her mite, we can feel generosity well up in our spirits despite our having empty purses. God's ways are not our ways; they transcend the natural, changing the humanly impossible into the divinely possible. "I was young and now I am old, yet I have never seen the righteous forsaken or their children begging bread. They are always generous and lend freely; their children will be blessed" (Ps. 37:25–26).

According to Paul, the test of our love centers on our generosity: "...I want to test the sincerity of your love by comparing it with the earnestness of others. For you know the grace of our Lord Jesus Christ, that though he was rich, yet for your sakes he became poor, so that you through his poverty might become rich" (2 Cor. 8:8–9).

The Master of generosity is Jesus, who exemplifies the generous heart and who models and imparts the riches of His grace so that we might follow His example of generosity toward others in order that they might also increase in generosity.

As missionaries, it is easy for us to take this passage as our challenge to lay down our lives for those on the mission field. But do we fail to consider our supporters or friends back home? Do we see supporters primarily in terms of their giving to us, not us to them? There are numerous directives in the New Testament to "prefer the brethren."

Galatians 6:10 challenges, "Therefore, as we have opportunity, let us do good to all people, especially to those who belong to the family of believers."

Jesus ministered to thousands, yet poured His life into the twelve disciples. Paul ministered to many, yet he focused on nurturing the churches to whom he was sent. We are to pour out our lives, as did Barb Mossberg in the Philippines, not only for those on the mission field but also for those back home. This includes even those who have never sent us money, who may never send us money, the ones from whom we never hear! If God puts them on our hearts, we must pray for their welfare, keep loving, keep being generous, keep pursuing. We are embraced by a pursuing God, often in spite of our response. We are compelled to do the same.

A team of supporters is not only for our benefit but for the world's benefit as well. God often uses our relationships as links to release laborers into the field. One missionary, Daniel, was supported by a couple for five years. During this time he sent them books, tapes, and various missions literature. After five years they decided to become missionaries themselves as a result of Daniel's input (and the Lord's). Yes, we may lose support because our supporters may join missions full time. We can't cling to their support. We cling to God and to our friends, not the dollars they may have. What is money compared to additional laborers being released into the harvest field?

This second pillar, generosity, expands friend raising into a lifestyle of giving and receiving with our friends and supporters—those who are cheering us on. Generosity provides a righteous foundation for us in support raising: seeking to serve and not to be served.

God's promises to us about generosity are powerful: "Now he who supplies seed to the sower and bread for food will also supply and increase your store of seed and will enlarge the harvest of your righteousness. You will be made rich in every way so that you can be generous on every occasion, and through us your generosity will result in thanksgiving to God. This service that you perform is not only supplying the needs of God's people but is also overflowing in many expressions of thanks to God" (2 Cor. 9:10–12).

Communication, the third pillar, is a practical way through which generosity and friend raising occur. Without communication we have little relationship with people. With it many doors of relationship are opened.

Notes

1. For information on Earl Pitts's teaching tapes, see the "Where to Go for More Help" section in the back of this book.
2. *Reader's Digest*, November 2001, p. 172.
3. George Barna, *Growing True Disciples* (Ventura, Calif.: Issachar Resources, 2000), pp. 61–62. For additional information on giving patterns, read "Evangelicals Are the Most Generous Givers, but Fewer Than 10% of Born Again Christians Give 10% to Their Church," *The Barna Update*, April 5, 2000, accessible on the Barna Research Web site, www.barna.org.

—

My friends hold open to me
hard places in their lives
that I must walk through
blindly, begging light.
My friends force open, in me,
doors I would not choose
or dare to enter.

—

— 4

THE THIRD PILLAR: COMMUNICATION

COMMUNICATION IS GOD'S DESIGN FOR INTERDEPENDENCE, evangelism, and friendship. As Paul points out, "...how shall they hear without a preacher?" (Rom. 10:14 KJV). As John says, "We proclaim to you what we have seen and heard, so that you also may have fellowship with us..." (1 John 1:3).

"I rejoice greatly in the Lord that at last you have renewed your concern for me. Indeed, you have been concerned, but you had no opportunity to show it. I am not saying this because I am in need, for I have learned to be content whatever the circumstances. I know what it is to be in need, and I know what it is to have plenty. I have learned the secret of being content in any and every situation, whether well fed or hungry, whether living in plenty or in want. I can do everything through him who gives me strength. Yet it was good of you to share in my troubles. Moreover, as you Philippians know, in the early days of your acquaintance with the gospel, when I set out from Macedonia, not one church shared with me in the matter

of giving and receiving, except you only; for even when I was in Thessalonica, you sent me aid again and again when I was in need. Not that I am looking for a gift, but I am looking for what may be credited to your account. I have received full payment and even more; I am amply supplied, now that I have received from Epaphroditus the gifts you sent...a fragrant offering, an acceptable sacrifice, pleasing to God. And my God will meet all your needs according to his glorious riches in Christ Jesus. To our God and Father be glory for ever and ever. Amen." (Phil. 4:10–20)

Paul's relationship with the Philippian church was founded on his generosity in ministering to them, discipling, disciplining, and nurturing them in their growth as Christians. When his generosity was fed back to him through their sacrificial giving, he in turn wrote a letter of thanks, love, and concern from prison in Rome. His statement, "You have been concerned, but you had no opportunity to show it," demonstrates an important principle: many people want to express their love in action but do not know how.

Communication is vital to our needs as missionaries. God has designed two methods of communication: solely with Him and with Him plus others.

Solely with Him

Sometimes the Holy Spirit speaks directly about someone's need to another, who responds in turn to the supernatural communication. Sometimes the call to be silent about needs is given to an organization. Overseas Missionary Fellowship (OMF) has this calling. They did not determine it on their own; it was God's calling. "[Hudson] Taylor firmly believed that the methods adopted were the God-given pattern for the CIM [now OMF]."[1] They have obeyed, and God blesses.

Even though Youth With A Mission as an organization does not have this calling, some individuals in YWAM do. Yet I believe that all of us at certain times will have specific situations where we receive this directive from God and experience the supernatural hand of God transcending the natural.

Our role model for this method is George Müller, who gained and gave millions of dollars to provide for orphans and other needy souls in Great Britain without ever asking for money. What he did do, however, was travel extensively to speak of the Lord's marvelous work in which he was privileged to share. His testimony spread far and wide. Without his mentioning specific needs, people realized the unique way he was used by God, and many supported the work. Communication was the key.

If God moved in this supernatural way for George Müller, can't He also move for us in the same way?

Of course! God is able to provide for "...all your needs according to his glorious riches in Christ Jesus" (Phil. 4:19).

However, He is not only the Author of supernatural communication but the Author of natural communication as well. Often His method for us alternates between, or combines, both the natural and supernatural.

With Him Plus Others

I believe that most of us primarily respond to naturally communicated needs, asking God for direction as we hear the needs. Mission Aviation Fellowship (MAF) states this approach: "It is the policy of MAF to honestly and accurately share the challenges and situations we face in all areas of our worldwide ministry. We make known needs and potential solutions so that friends can prayerfully consider sharing financially as the Lord leads and enables them. We believe motivation for all true giving comes as God moves in the hearts of people. Our part is to inform and give opportunity without imposing undue obligation or pressure."

How often do we give to a cause without first discovering the need through our eyes or ears? Imagine, if you will, your own pastor saying, "We're going to take an offering. Everyone, close your eyes. The Lord has shown me what the needs are, and I trust you'll all get the same message." Wouldn't you think he was a little crazy?

In addition, just as "you have not, because you ask not," we often "do not have" because we "do not ask" of one another. Imagine another circumstance, this one in a restaurant. You sit down and notice your place setting is without silverware. You want to respond in the most spiritual way and pray, "Lord, You know my needs. Please tell the waitress I need silverware. I don't want to have to ask." How absurd! There are times to pray and times to speak!

Certainly, telling your need to God alone is one method that God respects. However, it is neither more nor less spiritual to place our needs first before Him and then before others, offering them the opportunity not only to "bear one another's burdens" but also to "reap what they sow." Somehow we've set financial needs apart from other needs, finding it easier to ask for help only when we are piling up medical bills or needing some other specific financial assistance.

Once, in my own ministry, I uncovered some potentially disastrous calculations I had made on my quarterly tax payments: I was $2,000 short! I knew that by not acknowledging and dealing with the gnawing fear that I was underpaying as I went along, not responsibly figuring out what was "due to Caesar," I had sinned and the sin was catching up with me.

How could I possibly raise $2,000 for taxes? My first thought was—with a very creative newsletter, that's how!

I immediately sensed, however, that this was not God's answer for me. This was not a challenge to my clever know-how; it was a crisis between Him and me. I repented. When I asked for forgiveness and guidance, He prompted me not to contact my supporters but to phone my father.

Ask Dad for a loan? Was this God—or a joke?

My family was founded on financial responsibility, pulling oneself up by the bootstraps. In short, independence! Barnetts earn their own way; we don't borrow. But my many years as a missionary had taught me interdependence and humility.

I was to tell no one about the $2,000 shortage except my father. After days of fearfulness, I phoned Dad.

"Good timing!" he said. "I'm going to the bank this morning. I'll put the check in the mail today."

By the time I learned several months later that Dad had terminal cancer, he supposedly had only about two weeks to live. I flew home—my self-sufficient dad needed me. (My parents had divorced when I was five, and Dad had lived alone since then.) A hospice began helping Dad and me. He hated being in the hospital, so they arranged for a hospital bed to be placed in his home. Hospice workers came regularly and helped me care for him. Through God's grace, he lived for five months, giving valuable time for relationships with me and his other five children.

Soon after I began caring for Dad, I mustered up the courage to say, "Dad, I haven't forgotten about the $2,000. I haven't been able to pay it back yet, but I'm committed to pay it." He quickly responded, "Don't worry about it. You don't need to pay it back." For the first time in my life, my dad "fathered" me with finances (other than child support). The Lord, my Redeemer, had redeemed my sinful situation with the taxes and turned it into a giving-and-receiving exchange with Dad, a gift worth far more than $2,000, more than I could ask or think!

Though few are called to live solely by prayer, our creative God blows our culturally attuned minds sometimes with promptings like, "Call your father."

As with my dad, people often fail to respond to needs because they "have been concerned, but had no opportunity"—because they didn't know.

What Are We Communicating?

Paul learned to be content whatever his circumstances.

Careful not to manipulate others because of his needs, he was free to serve others by seeking their increase, not his own. It is easiest to raise support when we're not desperate for it. We can be free like George Müller, sharing the vision without demanding that people respond. Yet we will likely at some time find ourselves in the opposite situation, needing to raise support with a tinge of desperation. At those times we need God to impart contentment to us.

One summer on outreach to the Philippines, I strove to be content like Paul. It didn't work. One day I sensed the Lord saying, *Betty, you can't make yourself content. Only I can.* I then realized that it is a supernatural gift—a "secret," as Paul describes it, that only comes through relationship with and trust in God. Contentment comes from confidence in the Lord in each and every situation.

God brings us into different seasons: seasons of plenty and seasons of want. Both are important. A season of want, when our world seems upside down, may be a time of dynamic growth in our spiritual lives.

However, if a season of want becomes a lifestyle of want, something is wrong. We then need to ask the Holy Spirit to identify the hindrance. Have we been good stewards of our finances? Have we failed to communicate properly? Are we striving in the flesh and not in the Spirit? Is it lack of purity in our desire to see others benefit by giving to our share in God's work? Or is it discontent caused by the pressure of needs? (See chapter 7 for more hindrances.)

When God calls us, He also equips us. Our self-sufficiency is insufficient. Only He can provide a strong support base for our ministry. "I can do everything through him," Paul writes. The Philippians responded to Paul's circumstances in a right and loving way. Paul never said, "I wish I were tentmaking right now. Give me time and I'll get back on my feet." His response was, "It was good of you to share in my troubles" (Phil. 4:14).

Paul gave the faithful Philippian church due honor by stating truly that they were the only ones who gave. Sometimes we should let our few supporters know how precious they are to us, how crucial, how important in our lives and to our ministries. How will they know unless we tell them, unless we give them honor and say, "Hey, do you know that God used you profoundly? You were the only ones that gave to that project, and I want you to know how grateful I am."

Paul knew the Lord would credit the Philippians' heavenly account. Their gifts were a pleasing and appropriate sacrifice of honor to God, giving Him pleasure. God had prompted them to give. The worst thing Paul could have done was to refuse the gift. "Not that I am looking for a gift…" Understanding this principle will revolutionize our response to receiving gifts from supporters and affording them the opportunity to reap what they sow.

Warning: we must be careful never to dangle this or any other verse of promise like a carrot before our supporters, using God's Word to manipulate. It is simply an after-the-fact promise of thanks, because God's system of finances frees us both to give and to receive.

Jesus said, "...all men will know that you are my disciples, if you love one another" (John 13:35). He also prayed a powerful prayer for all believers in John 17:23: "May they be brought to complete unity to let the world know that you sent me and have loved them even as you have loved me." These verses refer to love lived out by good works, interdependence and unity, and a literal linking arms together in community—not in independent living.

People really do want to be involved in our lives. The world is big; the needs are great. Many people who have no access to overseas ministry would respond positively to a trustworthy avenue for personal involvement in world missions—if they only knew how.

Be careful not to manipulate—watch for hidden hindrances and then communicate!

This third pillar, communication, is best built on a lifestyle similar to Paul's: one of love and ministry for those he was writing to and visiting. The communication of our needs may be solely with Him at times and, at other times, with Him plus others. Each has its place; neither is more spiritual than the other.

Prayer with promises, the fourth pillar, summons us to dependence upon God, our ultimate source of provision.

Note

1. Daniel W. Bacon, *From Faith to Faith: The Influence of Hudson Taylor on the Faith Missions Movement* (Littleton, Colo.: OMF Books, 1984), p. 31.

—

A Christian is someone
who lives beyond his or her
own abilities and understanding.

—

THE FOURTH PILLAR: PRAYER WITH PROMISES

PERHAPS IT GOES WITHOUT SAYING THAT PRAYER IS essential throughout all friend-raising activities. But perhaps it will go without prayer if it's not said! It seems so easy and natural for those of us in "spiritual work" to have much of our ministry designated as spiritual while other parts of our ministry are more secular.

Having experienced both means of friend raising—both by the flesh and by the Spirit—I know the temptation to venture out without prayer and without the undergirding of the Lord. But we are colaborers with Him, not in our own strength. It is "'…not by might nor by power, but by my Spirit,' says the LORD Almighty" (Zech. 4:6). We periodically need Paul's prodding: "After beginning with the Spirit, are you now trying to attain your goal by human effort?" (Gal. 3:3)

Chapters 2–4 describe three of the pillars of support raising: friend raising, generosity, and communication. Yet the roof will cave in without the fourth pillar: prayer and a desperate dependence upon God. Nick, a YWAM leader and teacher of fund-raising, learned this lesson through a painful experience. He was asked by Loren Cunningham, founder of YWAM, to share his support-raising principles at a staff meeting. He complied. However, during the two months following, his family's support dried up. God finally had his attention when they were $5,000 in debt, and Nick prayed for understanding. He was reminded of the staff meeting and sensed the Lord saying, "You shared My principles but gave Me no credit. You took the glory for yourself." Duly corrected, Nick repented.

Soon after, someone surprised him with an envelope containing a $5,000 check from a faraway donor.

Nick quickly phoned the donor to thank him. The man said, "The money is part of our tithe from an inheritance and should have come to you two months ago. Somehow it got held up. We're not sure how or why."

"I am!" cried Nick. "'Not by might nor by power, but by my Spirit,' says the LORD Almighty." And Nick gave all the glory to God!

Our long-term success in support raising or friend raising is dependent upon God being our source of wisdom and ideas: His strength when we're weak, His encouragement when we're discouraged, and His spiritual tactics for battle against the Enemy, who will barrage us with his hellish arsenal, often in unexpected times, places, and through unexpected people.

As described in Ephesians 6, all aspects of spiritual warfare are important, but the capstone is described in verse 18 and is key for support raising: "And pray in the Spirit on all occasions with all kinds of prayers and requests. With this in mind, be alert and always keep on praying for all the saints." The following are verses I've found helpful in battles— reminders of the Lord's promises to us: "...asking God to fill you with the knowledge of his will through all spiritual wisdom and understanding...in order that you may live a life

worthy of the Lord and may please him in every way: bea
ing fruit in every good work, growing in the knowledge of
God, being strengthened with all power…" (Col. 1:9–11).

The first element of spiritual warfare is "truth." Below are
some favorite scriptures—line after line of God's truth for
prayer purposes and meditation, a fitting arsenal against the
Enemy's lies. Reminder cards of significant verses may help
encourage you and strengthen you. These verses begin with
prayer cries of our initial fear and trembling. They then progress
to emphasize God's faithfulness, strength, and promises.

Discouragement Antidotes

"I call on the LORD in my distress, and he answers me"
(Ps. 120:1).

"I lift up my eyes to the hills—where does my help come
from? My help comes from the LORD, the Maker of heaven
and earth. He will not let your foot slip—he who watches
over you will not slumber…he will watch over your life; the
LORD will watch over your coming and going both now and
forevermore" (Ps. 121:1–3, 7–8).

"Lord, I have so many enemies! Lead me to do your will;
make your way plain for me to follow.…You bless those who
obey you, Lord; your love protects them like a shield" (Ps.
5:8, 12, Good News).

"I sought the LORD, and he answered me; he delivered me
from all my fears. Those who look to him are radiant; their
faces are never covered with shame.…The angel of the LORD
encamps around those who fear him, and he delivers them"
(Ps. 34:4–5, 7).

"Praise be to the LORD, my Rock, who trains my hands for
war, my fingers for battle" (Ps. 144:1).

"Let us then approach the throne of grace with confidence, so that we may receive mercy and find grace to help

us in our time of need....God is not unjust; he will not forget your work and the love you have shown him as you have helped his people and continue to help them....Imitate those who through faith and patience inherit what has been promised" (Heb. 4:16; 6:10, 12).

"I cried out to God for help; I cried out to God to hear me. When I was in distress, I sought the Lord....You are the God who performs miracles; you display your power among the peoples....You led your people like a flock..." (Ps. 77:1–2, 14, 20).

"...The LORD is faithful to all his promises and loving toward all he has made" (Ps. 145:13).

"Therefore, my dear brothers, stand firm. Let nothing move you. Always give yourselves fully to the work of the Lord, because you know that your labor in the Lord is not in vain" (1 Cor. 15:58).

"The one who calls you is faithful and he will do it" (1 Thess. 5:24).

"Now to him who is able to do immeasurably more than all we ask or imagine, according to his power that is at work within us" (Eph. 3:20).

"Summon your power, O God; show us your strength, O God, as you have done before" (Ps. 68:28).

"I waited patiently for the LORD; he turned to me and heard my cry. He lifted me out of the slimy pit, out of the mud and mire; he set my feet on a rock...a firm place to stand. He put a new song in my mouth, a hymn of praise to our God. Many will see and fear and put their trust in the LORD.... 'I desire to do your will, O my God; your law is within my heart.' I proclaim righteousness in the great assembly [through newsletters, speaking, etc.]; I do not seal my lips....I speak of your faithfulness and salvation. I do not conceal your love and your truth from the great assembly" (Ps. 40:1–3, 8–10).

"This is love for God: to obey his commands. And his commands are not burdensome" (1 John 5:3).

"I thank Christ Jesus our Lord, who has given me strength, that he considered me faithful, appointing me to his service" (1 Tim. 1:12).

"If I must boast, I will boast of the things that show my weakness....But he said to me, 'My grace is sufficient for you, for my power is made perfect in weakness.' Therefore I will boast all the more gladly about my weaknesses, so that Christ's power may rest on me. That is why, for Christ's sake, I delight in weaknesses, in insults, in hardships, in persecutions, in difficulties. For when I am weak, then I am strong" (2 Cor. 11:30; 12:9–10).

"Blessed are all who fear the LORD, who walk in his ways. You will eat the fruit of your labor; blessings and prosperity will be yours" (Ps. 128:1–2).

"Fight the good fight of the faith" (1 Tim 6:12). Support raising requires deep faith!

"Endure hardship with us like a good soldier of Christ Jesus" (2 Tim 2:3).

"He has preserved our lives and kept our feet from slipping....You...tested us; you refined us like silver....We went through fire and water, but you brought us to a place of abundance" (Ps. 66:9–12).

"And in him you too are being built together to become a dwelling in which God lives by his Spirit" (Eph. 2:22).

"We...remember...your work produced by faith, your labor prompted by love, and your endurance inspired by hope in our Lord Jesus Christ" (1 Thess. 1:3).

"If you fully obey the LORD your God and carefully follow all his commands I give you today, the LORD your God will set you high above all the nations on earth" (Deut. 28:1).

"Now to him who is able to establish you...so that all nations might believe and obey him" (Rom. 16:25–26).

"Trust in the LORD and do good; dwell in the land and enjoy safe pasture. Delight yourself in the LORD and he will give you the desires of your heart. Commit your way to the LORD; trust in him and he will do this: he will make your righteousness shine like the dawn, the justice of your cause like the noonday sun. Be still before the LORD and wait patiently for him; do not fret....Wait for the LORD and keep his way. He will exalt you to inherit the land..." (Ps. 37:3–7, 34).

May we learn to live a life of prayer and faith, with Scripture and God's promises to us as a foundation. In this regard we can draw valuable lessons from Hudson Taylor's life and work. He reminds us that missions is powerfully linked with prayer. Daniel Bacon, former U.S. Director of Overseas Missionary Fellowship (OMF), states that, "Gratefully, technological developments have provided many helpful tools for missionary work, along with organizational structures that greatly facilitate the recruitment, sending, maintenance, and support of mission personnel. But...tools and organizations can never substitute for God's power which comes alone in answer to prayer...dependence upon God in prayer is the ultimate way for doing spiritual work."[1]

The fourth pillar of prayer with promises will either be our point of greatest strength or, if we don't pray, our point of greatest weakness. We will either walk into the land that He has promised to us or fall flat on our faces in the dry, sandy desert, parched and wasted away.

With all four pillars in place, we can now explore practical means of living a friend-raising lifestyle. God will give you additional ideas, inspired by His heart of love and caring for His people. Feel free to make notes throughout the next chapter as ideas come to your mind.

Note

1. Daniel W. Bacon, *From Faith to Faith: The Influence of Hudson Taylor on the Faith Missions Movement* (Littleton, Colo.: OMF Books, 1984), pp. 185–186.

—

Friendship is abused
either by our demands upon it
or by our demeaning of it;
it may die as certainly
of glut as of starvation.

—

– 6

FRIEND RAISING
MADE PRACTICAL

GOD'S WAYS OF FRIEND RAISING ARE LOVING AND personal, leading us to levels of intimacy from highly private to more institutional. His methods are not always comfortable but are always generous.

The most helpful guideline for me in friend raising has been to continually ask the question, "If I were they, how would I want to be treated?" Or, in Jesus' familiar words, "So in everything, do to others what you would have them do to you…" (Matt. 7:12). Remember to imagine yourself in others' shoes to help determine how you'll practically walk out your friend raising.

It is good for us to share ourselves at each level, beyond our level of comfort. We too often put up walls and hide ourselves behind masks. The walls need to be replaced with bridges; the masks, with faces. We need to be available; we need to be real; and we need to be generous.

Generosity toward others is our gift to God. It costs us something. King David said, "I will not sacrifice to the LORD my God burnt offerings that cost me nothing" (2 Sam. 24:24).

If we love Him, it is our joy to give to the Lord by giving to His people. As we look to Him for His heart of generosity, we can expect a growing number of "generosity nudges" from the Holy Spirit, prompting us to express generosity in a variety of ways. These nudges will occur with people who *have* supported us, people who *will* support us, and people who will *never* support us. Generosity is not based on any potential return benefit but on a freely flowing heart, sensitive to Him.

As our heavenly Father shared Himself with us through the gift of His Son, sharing ourselves with others is the most generous gift we can offer. In each case it comes in a different wrapping.

As I look back over more than twenty years of living in this faith/support lifestyle, two things rise to the top as having had the greatest impact on my building a lasting missionary support team: the gifts I've given and the visits I've made. In both cases we may think, "But I can't afford to…" I would suggest that it's just the opposite: we can't afford *not* to!

Face to Face

Visit one on one, face to face. (This can include not only your visiting others but also friends' visiting you on the field, if possible!) This is the most significant and effective means of friend raising. Even a brief meal shared with friends can have more impact than years of personal letters, "…I do not want to use paper and ink. Instead I hope to visit you and talk with you face to face, so that our joy may be complete" (2 John 12).

Spend time with people, especially in their homes. Share a meal, a cup of tea, a five-minute chat, a short prayer. Share a feast. Biblical feasts had special significance, in both the physical realm and the spiritual. Lives change when Christians break bread together. Look for "memory makers." These are moments shared in friend raising that you'll treasure for years to come. Create a memory by taking a walk with a friend. Knit your lives together. Be there. It may pave the way for others to be there for you in your time of need. Sometimes only a moment totally focused is important—even life-changing. Remember the listening lessons from chapter 2.

In addition, when appropriate, stay in people's homes, sharing a slice of daily life with them. Those precious moments together can last a lifetime. Remembering that your goal is to bless your friend, bring a gift with you and be a sensitive houseguest, considerate of your host's routines and preferences.

Many mission agencies have furlough policies that encourage their missionaries to visit friends and supporters every three or four years. However, I advise that it be done more often, if possible. Friendships lapse with infrequent face-to-face contact. Our joy is linked to our visits, as Paul describes: "…I want very much to see you, in order to share a spiritual blessing with you to make you strong. What I mean is that both you and I will be helped at the same time, you by my faith and I by yours" (Rom. 1:11–12, Good News).

Visits also give us opportunities to serve, even briefly, in our home churches. It's helpful to know our strengths and abilities, offering to give according to our giftings, whether it is teaching Sunday-school classes, serving, preaching, or providing a listening ear. Give abundantly of your "plenty" while you have the opportunity, not as the super-spiritual authority but as a servant, offering help.

Difficulty arises when we feel restrained from visiting due to either limited finances or pressing needs on the field. However, the priority of visits must be understood. Our ability to serve long-term on the field is directly linked to the health of our relationships back home. We may need to pray for a response similar to "…out of our intense longing we made every effort to see you" (1 Thess. 2:17).

Telephone

The next best thing to being there is a phone call. Friendships deepen with the sound of a voice, shared prayer requests, current news (good and bad), mutual love acknowledged, and commitment reaffirmed.

Budget a generous amount for phone expenses. With low-cost long-distance phone cards, this is a relatively inexpensive way to keep in touch with people. Practice listening skills over the phone. Set a goal of calling several supporters each month, maybe one a week (on Saturdays or Sundays, when people are likely to be home, remembering the time zone they are in so that you don't phone when they're sleeping!). Ask God to bring the right people to mind and expect surprising fruit!

Friends in Florida once sent me an unusual gift, a bright yellow ball, with a note: "As the sun rises in Florida, know that we're praying for you." Touched by the gesture, I phoned them to ask, "What's going on in your lives?" I also wanted to know what they had been praying for me. First they shared some special joys in their lives, then what they had been praying. They had been right on target, and we were all encouraged—a marvelous phone conversation, a pocket of friend raising in an otherwise ordinary day.

Phone someone to say how special and timely his or her gift was. When I was business manager for Lamb's Players, we received a $1,000 check—not our usual contribution! I phoned the donors and said, "We want to thank you. Your gift was incredible! It was very timely, and we greatly appreciate it." The wife answered, "You know, we've given away thousands of dollars and, until now, we've never received a phone call of thanks."

As an indirect result of that spontaneous phone call, the couple eventually joined Lamb's Players' board of directors, knitting us all together for future ministry.

Written Messages

Handwritten messages, whether notes, letters, or postcards, make people feel special. Newsletters are also an excellent means of communication (see chapter 10), but I don't know anyone who receives a missionary newsletter who does not first look for a personalized written message at the end. Often we procrastinate, feeling that we must write a lengthy letter about all we've been involved in lately to "get credit" for writing. If that's your tendency, you can always send postcards for quick thank-you notes: simply address the card and write the date of the gift and amount where the postage stamp will be placed. Carry it around with you until you have a moment for a quick note. The point is not to produce a mininewsletter but to express thanks.

The importance of saying thank you cannot be overestimated. It is the most important aspect of communication for us. If we fail to express our thanks appropriately, we may never receive another gift from that person, and we damage the relationship.

I know a Christian executive who travels the world over. He carries postcards to send whenever he wants to remind someone of his love and prayers. The Jews for Jesus ministry sends periodic handwritten postcards to each donor. I've been supporting them for more than twenty years and have received many postcards expressing gratitude and current prayer requests. The personal touch makes a difference.

Most of us would rather receive two postcards a year from friends (whether a missionary or not!) than twelve printed newsletters chock full of information. We all appreciate personal notes written in our friend's handwriting (assuming we can read it!). Develop the rewarding habit of writing brief, spontaneous notes to whomever the Lord brings to mind. When He prompts you to pray for someone, let the person know.

Include an encouraging Scripture verse to give a spiritual boost to both giver and receiver. It may be a verse you read in your devotional reading or one that the Lord pointed out to you as a gift for your friend.

We don't have to write much: "It's the thought [put into words] that counts!"

Encourage supporters by reminding them of their significant partnership role in ministry. They are as much a part of the missionary endeavor as you are. Bernie May, former U.S. Division Director of Wycliffe Bible Translators, blessed supporters and friends of Wycliffe missionaries for years through his monthly thank-you letters. I've heard comments from many recipients that his letters made them feel so good, so privileged to be part of Wycliffe's ministry. May we all be inspired by God to bless others through our letters!

E-mail

Cyberspace is a means of instant communication, the next best thing to phoning for many people (and easier and less costly). E-mail offers great potential for being very helpful, or at times, annoying and even potentially harmful.

E-mails are very helpful
- to get out news and prayer requests quickly,
- to instantly reach many people (even those with limited access to mail) with minimal effort and expense,
- to personally connect with close friends, family, and home church,
- to share digital photos of ourselves in ministry, fresh from the field.

E-mails may be counterproductive if
- they're the only way we communicate with friends,
- they include attachments that are carriers of computer viruses,

- they take extra work to access and open because of excess size or formatting incompatibility.

Any time you make it more difficult for your reader to access your letter, you will lose part of your audience. Because not everyone has a high-speed connection, if you are attaching or embedding photos in an e-mail, they should be as low-resolution as possible to still look good. Keep size and compatibility in mind for other attachments as well.

Aim to minimize the frequency of sending mass e-mails, but when you do, use the "blind copy" function to protect peoples' privacy. If it is not feasible to send each e-mail individually, consider sending them in smaller groups; they will be less likely to end up in the junk mail folders of recipients who use filters. Also, all e-newsletters should include an opt-out clause so that recipients who no longer wish to be on the e-mailing list can let you know to remove them.

Whenever possible, personalize each e-mail with an opening sentence or two, written directly to that person or persons, such as:

> Dear Joe and Susan,
> It was great to hear of your recent family news—you must be thrilled by all that God has done for you. Below is an update on me. Thank you again for partnering with me in this ministry!
> Love, Betty
>
> *Ministry Update from Betty Barnett (month/year)*

Then simply include the same primary news to each person. Avoid making people feel as if they're part of a mass audience. Remember, the more people feel you've written specifically to them, the more likely they'll read your letter, whether by e-mail or by regular mail.

Web Sites

Internet web sites can be an excellent way to keep your friends, family, church, and supporters updated. As with e-mail, web sites are an easy and efficient way to instantly share news, prayer requests, stories, and photographs. Along with your mission statement and specifics about your ministry or organization, include your current activities. Many people post a section of frequently requested information, such as their address and phone number and their monthly financial needs. You might choose to include interesting articles, pictures, or information about the country or community where you are ministering, as well as links to some of your favorite relevant web sites. Keep in mind that interactive features promote relationships. Some web hosts allow your visitors to post messages on a message board or make donations online with the ease of automatic bank transfers. You can also include links to your latest newsletter and to your e-mail address.

A web site can serve as an enhancement to your other forms of contact. For example, you might briefly mention a recent trip in your newsletter or e-mail update and then include your web-site address (or a link to it at the end of your e-mail) where friends can peruse photos and a more detailed account of the trip at their leisure.

To complement your web site or e-newsletters, a digital camera might be a good investment, especially if you do not have access to a scanner. Though more expensive up front, digital cameras save money on film and developing fees and make it easy for you to keep your site current.

There are numerous approaches to web creation and design, from the very basic do-it-yourself method to professional design and creation companies, who will do it for you. Your organization may be able to assist you. (For example, see www.ywamconnect.com.) You may also be able to locate an individual or ministry who would assist you on a gift, discount, or trade basis.

If you are new at web-site production, ask friends for recommendations of good sites, or go to a search engine and put in keywords such as "missionary," "Christian out-reach," or the name of a ministry you are familiar with. Looking at some of the sites that come up will give you an idea of the breadth of possibilities, as well as what works—and doesn't—for your particular needs.

Regardless of how you build it, remember that your web site is all about relationships. As visitors come to your web site, they are building relationship with you by participating in and learning about your life and ministry. This is an important reason to make sure that your site is personal and frequently updated. Always include the date of the last update so that visitors know that the site is active and closely followed by you. A site that is current and always changing has much more relationship potential.

Church Communication

Send items back home regularly to be included in the church bulletin or monthly church newsletters. Also send potential bulletin inserts. (Have them camera-ready copy, if possible.)

If you have access to a video camera, consider videos showing sites and scenes from your everyday mission life, such as "a day in the life of a missionary family." It could be a delightful treat for your church, giving more exposure to your experiences and needs.

If videos are impossible, consider sending an audio cassette or a photo presentation on CD or DVD, to be played for the congregation during church services. An audio cassette could be a simple five-minute message sharing greetings, prayer requests, and gratitude for their love and prayer support.

Some pastors have arranged live phone calls to a missionary during a Sunday morning church service, with the congregation listening through the church's sound system. This can be enormously encouraging for all involved.

Gift Giving

Giving appropriate gifts is a wonderful, tangible expression of generosity, love, and the desire to serve.

Proverbs 18:16 says, "A gift opens the way for the giver and ushers him into the presence of the great."

Any time is the right time to send a gift when the Lord gives a specific idea for a group or individual. Pay attention to His nudges. When we stay sensitive to the Lord and to the needs of our supporters, we will no doubt be prompted to send a card or gift at just the right moment.

I watch for appropriate items that my mission organization sells, and I select different Christmas gifts each year for supporters and others I want to bless. I also watch for small, practical items while on field trips, knowing that colorful, international gifts impart the flavor of the culture and help my supporters feel a part of my experiences.

Christian books and CDs or cassette tapes make excellent gifts, nurturing and discipling as well as expressing our love. The Lord touches and changes lives through literature and recorded messages.

One generosity nudge from the Lord regarding cassette tapes gave surprising results: I sent a set of Earl Pitts's tapes on finances to a friend in California. I called my friend almost a year later. She had planned on visiting me in Hawaii but never did. I asked why, and she surprised me with, "It's because of those tapes you sent me."

"Would you please explain that to me?!" I blurted.

She went on, "Soon after receiving them, I spent a whole afternoon listening to them and was so convicted by the Lord about my spending habits that I realized I had no business going to Hawaii until I was more stable financially. Right now, I'm working on eliminating my debts, and by the end of this year, I should be debt-free for the first time in many years! Then I'll come to Hawaii. I'll even have frequent flyer passes to be able to fly free!"

I was so grateful for the nudge that had produced significant fruit in my friend's life. She has not been a financial supporter of mine for many years. I didn't send the tapes to receive results for myself. My simple act of generosity was with a heart of, "Not that I am looking for a gift, but I am looking for what may be credited to your account" (Phil. 4:17).

Another generosity nudge involved a T-shirt. One evening just before the Korean Olympics, as I was taking laundry out of the clothes dryer, a woman who was staying in the guest room next door came out to chat. She was on her way to Korea to join evangelistic efforts at the Olympics. As I began folding a T-shirt that had recently been given to me, I showed it to her. It was solid black, with a beautiful four-color graphic printed on the front with "Seoul, Korea Olympics" and John 3:16 in Korean written in vivid red ink on the back. It had become one of my favorite T-shirts.

As I showed it to her, I sensed one of those nudges. I struggled silently as I argued with God, *But it's my favorite!* I pushed aside the desire to cling to "my possession" and gave it to her. She initially said, "Oh, no, you can't..." but then graciously received it. She wrote soon after the Olympics, "You don't know what that night meant to me. You'll never know..." She later wrote, "Just wanted you to know that the T-shirt has raised a lot of conversations here in the States when I wear it, and I am glad to share with whoever will listen! So you see, you gave a gift that keeps on giving. Thanks for your kindness. I will never forget it."

Awareness

A generous act of communication can be simply noticing someone who isn't doing well, who perhaps is ill or has lost a loved one and who needs a note or a phone call from someone who cares. Perhaps we read about the person in the church newsletter. Not on our mailing list? It doesn't matter! God will bless us, supply our needs, and add to us so we can be even more generous, reflecting the character of His Son.

Where to Begin

Perhaps you're asking, "How do I begin? Where do I start friend raising?" The answer is to begin with what you have, not with what you don't have. As with the loaves and fish, Jesus took the pittance of a little boy's lunch and turned it into something spectacular—the multiplication factor was at work! Through this circumstance, Jesus essentially asked the disciples, "What do you have?" He then took what they had and gave thanks for it. They knew it wasn't enough (as you do). But they gave it to Him, and He blessed it, gave it back to them, and multiplied it as they went out in obedience. We too are to give Him what little we have, thank Him for it, ask Him to bless it—and then handle it well, in faith and in deed. We offer Him the small, medium, or large list of friends and acquaintances we have, beginning there and relating to those people first. Be careful not to despise small beginnings. If we handle well and are faithful with the little amount we have—whether money, possessions, or relationships—more will be entrusted to us. Conversely, if we handle poorly that which we have, it will likely shrivel (see Luke 16:10–12).

Perhaps you've lost touch with people by lack of communication, either theirs or yours. Pray about those people with whom you regret having lost touch. Ask God, the One who seeks that which is lost, to restore your lost relationships. If you don't have current addresses, ask God to help you find them. Perhaps persons will come to mind who may have them.

The self-evaluation found in the "Helps and Forms" section at the end of this book is a helpful tool. Begin your friend-raising process by completing this form, feeling free to adapt it to fit your situation or mission group. This evaluation also includes making a list of "People You Can Communicate With." Additional sample forms, such as the Friendship Record, are helpful for compiling names, addresses, and personal information (birthdays, etc.). Some of these people may be dear friends and others may be acquaintances. Who knows what is in store for you and them in the future?

As you fill out the form and compile your list (start with your Christmas card list, if that helps), ask the Lord to expand your borders, both in your faith for His network of support and also in widening the realm and depth of your relationships. Ephesians 2:22 describes His purposes for us well: "And in him you too are being built together to become a dwelling in which God lives by his Spirit."

How to Ask

"They did not do as we expected, but they gave themselves first to the Lord and then to us in keeping with God's will" (2 Cor. 8:5). A key principle: encourage people to first ask the Lord and then to respond to us according to His will. In other words, our "asking" includes asking them to ask the Lord and do only what they feel right about doing. We only want their obedience to Him, not to us. We don't want responses out of emotion or obligation, but from the Lord's leading. Generosity only operates in freedom. If freedom of choice is removed, generosity no longer exists. It does not exist within the law—the "have to"—but it bursts through the law, breaking the framework of obligation.

This verse zeroes in on unfulfilled expectations. Often our expectations will be faulty. We will continually be surprised by those who give and those who don't. The very people you most expect to give may be the least likely, and the ones you least expect to give may surprise you with their rich generosity. Be careful not to select the people you think *should* give. God does the selecting; we do the communicating. When we do the selecting, it becomes a "work of the flesh," and we find disappointment.

Many people prefer investing in projects such as a computer, car, boat for river travel for ministry purposes, goats, oxen, etc. They're able to see their finances help in a tangible way. The farmers who sent vegetable seeds to Barb Mossberg invested in a way that was just as appropriate, if not more so, than money. Consider giving your friends and supporters a list of ways they could pray about participating in projects in which you are involved.

You Are Cordially Invited...

In many areas of our lives, we respond by invitation only. We have dinner at a friend's house when we've been invited. We often get involved in projects through the invitation of a friend who's already involved. We come to the living God through His personal invitation. I call this principle "you are cordially invited." The more personal, the more specific, and the more "inviting" (not manipulative) the invitation is, the greater the likelihood of response.

You may wonder why a team of workers or supporters is not coming together. It may be that you have not given a very specific or attractive invitation. One group of missionaries in the Philippines began staff support raising based on relationships. They visited homes of friends and acquaintances, presenting their mission's activities and their personal ministry role. They included simple but personal invitations for involvement through ministry partnership. Many of the Filipino staff were quickly able to raise their support simply by going out and meeting with people individually.

I once did an informal survey of our YWAM staff in Kona, Hawaii. I learned that each person had joined the staff through a very personal and specific invitation from another YWAM staff member who said something like, "Would you pray about coming on staff in a particular department and doing this job?" Many missionary supporters join ministry teams in the same manner. Potential supporters may simply need to be personally asked, "Would you pray about supporting me monthly? It could range anywhere from $5 a month to $100, or however God leads you. But please don't feel pressured; it's simply an invitation to pray."

Often this key principle of personal invitation is missing. We give mass-meeting-style presentations in our newsletters, then we wonder what's gone wrong. However, if we had taken those same words and written them by hand in a letter, the effectiveness could rise dramatically because all of us respond better to personal invitations. If someone I know sends me a handwritten letter, asking me to pray about involvement, he or she can be reasonably sure I'll pray about it. When we receive a personal request, we are more likely to consider that we serve a generous God who may be looking for an opportunity to encourage and support a friend through us. "Indeed, you have been concerned, but you had no opportunity…" (Phil. 4:10).

After the father of one missionary family visited various friends, describing their ministry involvement and support needs, he gave personal invitations for ministry partnership to twenty people. Seventeen out of twenty became monthly financial supporters because of that invitation. Just as positive response occurred in the Philippines, it can happen in any culture.

Heart attitude is most important in our relationships. If we have an attitude of mutual giving and receiving with potential supporters, they will know it. If we're just there trying to get their money, they will know that, too! I've personally supported some individuals from my church who only communicated with me when I sent money. Then when they left the ministry, I never heard from them again. I was left with a hollow, empty feeling. The money should be a by-product, not the core, of the relationship.

Time of Testing

An additional element is one of a "testing time." As banks often will not consider issuing a loan to a new business until it has been in operation for at least three years, many of our friends and family may stand back and watch. They want to know if our new zeal for missions will last. They want long-term investment, as do the banks. They want their money to make a difference. They don't want to be involved in a fling. With some people your persistence in relationship and sharing the word of your testimony over time will make the difference. It may take many years for some, only months for others.

Priorities in Relationships

Who are the most important people with whom you should have ongoing communication? Those with "big bucks"? Hopefully, by now it's obvious that that's not my recommendation.

An obvious priority group is those who have *pledged* prayer and financial support. Their prayers and gifts comprise a strong statement of commitment. As they are committed to us, we must be committed to them with updates, reports, and expressions of gratitude and love. Be careful not to discount those who have made a prayer commitment. Their investment may be even more valuable than the financial ones!

Include in this high-priority group others who are close to your heart—family members, close friends (whether they support you or not), and also significant people in your church, such as the pastor, missions committee, elders, etc. We often need the Holy Spirit to help us know who the most significant people are. Out of the potential group of people with whom we should keep in contact, which should we give our greatest attention—perhaps with bimonthly personal notes or letters and Christmas gifts? Which ones should simply receive semiannual newsletters? Allow God to lead, and as the years go on, you will have a network of relationships that God has woven together.

In time a core group of people will emerge from this broad network of relationships as your "life-support" team. Ask the Lord to help you identify the people He intends to support you in this more intimate way. These close, committed friends will hold you accountable for all aspects of your life and ministry, and they will strengthen and encourage you in special ways. With them you can be fully honest and transparent while still being loved.

The small but very special group of people who are my life-support team ask me hard questions as well as listen to me. They are not only my cheerleaders but also my protectors, helping me walk uprightly and in strength when I am filled with weakness. For example, over ten years ago, as the first edition of *Friend Raising* was about to be published, I was hospitalized with life-threatening pneumonia. Within twenty-four hours of my core team's being notified, prayer was ignited through them to nearly two thousand others, sending up a tremendous wave of intercession on my behalf. My medical condition quickly turned around. The doctors, who had tried every possible medical treatment with no response, were amazed. This was the most concrete form of life support I could ever imagine. My brush with death was reversed through the multiplied prayers of my life-support team. Many people who had never heard of me before were stirred to pray through those closest to me who cared the most. My prayer is that you, too, would have this life-support team come around you in your ministry.

Sending

"How, then, can they call on the one they have not believed in?…How can they hear without someone preaching to them? And how can they preach unless they are sent?" (Rom. 10:14–15).

Paul doesn't ask, "How can they preach unless they go?" but rather, "How can they preach unless they are sent?" Paul implies others' involvement in launching the missionary into service as a strong link, perhaps even a prerequisite, to a missionary's ability to preach the gospel. The aspect of "sending" a missionary is a significant step in the support-raising process, one that deserves attention.

The local church in the body of Christ is a sending vehicle. Too often, churches say to the missionary, "Go on your way now. Be warm and well fed…" without taking any responsibility for the missionary's needs. Sometimes churches don't understand their role, and we may be able to help by offering suggestions or requests. The book *Serving as Senders* is an excellent resource. (For more information see "Where to Go for More Help" in the back of this book.) You could buy *Serving as Senders* as a gift for your church to help them grow in this area.

Sending is far more than just giving financial support; it includes many aspects of literal blessing—counsel and advice, emotional support and encouragement, as well as equipping through discipleship and practical training for missionary service. In addition, the church can give spiritual blessing through the laying on of hands and prayers of the pastor and elders, ongoing prayer support after the missionary's departure, and material blessing through financial support and sending physical goods helpful on the mission field.

But how does this happen? What if you haven't been strongly involved in a local church that could send you? Perhaps you have broken relationships with your church and need to repent and walk in reconciliation. Perhaps you need to consider delaying your departure to the mission field for six months to two years, until you have built up a loving and nurturing church relationship. The church needs to have an understanding of who you are, your calling, and your gifts, or they will be hindered in helping you "go." Generally this comes out of a lifestyle of having invested your life in them and in pouring your life into the life of the church, with a heart of generosity and service.

One long-term missionary family returned to the U.S. from their field ministry in the Middle East to reestablish the relationship with their local church. They felt that the Lord told them to return to invest two years in their church. The husband of this couple had been known by the church as "the pastor's rebel son." He recommitted his life to the Lord at his father's funeral. But soon after that, he entered missionary service overseas. The church had little relationship with him until he returned with his family. It was a difficult decision for the couple and a trying season for them, as their hearts ached to be back on the mission field. However, they were convinced that their future missionary service was directly linked to their investment in the church.

How can we nurture the process of sending? First, by practicing the principle of submission to your spiritual authority. You are to submit your missionary plans for their confirmation of the call (not their decision, as was discussed earlier). Your submission comes out of relationship with the pastor and the church leadership team.

One California couple felt the Lord was leading them into missions, and they phoned to share their heart with their pastor. They told him what they believed God was saying to them and said that they were submitting this to him as their spiritual authority. His response was immediate: "The Bible has already given all of us the mandate to 'go into all the world and preach the gospel.' If you believe God is calling you to go, I would say that agrees with Scripture and I would confirm it. I will pray for you—but specifically in the area of timing or any concerns the Lord may reveal."

If your pastor or elders don't mention it, feel free to ask them to have a corporate time of blessing during the Sunday morning church service soon before your departure for the field.

"...Fan into flame the gift of God, which is in you through the laying on of my hands" (2 Tim. 1:6). The spiritual blessing through the laying on of hands is an important and meaningful gift from your church leaders that helps release your ministry gift. It also makes a public statement to the congregation of the church leadership's endorsement and support, as well as encourages ongoing prayer commitments.

A second area through which you may encourage the sending process is by asking the church for practical help: perhaps picking up the cost of newsletter printing, mailing, postage, and labor; perhaps a "send-off shower" of physical and spiritual blessing (giving them a list of practical needs for the field or having a "money tree" to help cover your relocation expenses).

What if you have submitted to your church leadership and yet there is no initiative to "send" you? Perhaps you will be like Bruce Olson, a missionary who left the U.S. at the age of nineteen for South America against the wishes of many and without the support of any. Yet he had the Lord's strong directive to do so. His story is told in his powerful book, *Bruchko*.

Individual friends are also a strong part of the sending process. Their encouragement, prayers, and support are priceless. Through an ongoing prayer commitment, with mutual prayer requests and answers, their life-giving support goes far beyond measure. Some thoughtful friends may want to periodically send you "care packages" of items available only from your home country. Treats such as your favorite packaged foods—candy, macaroni and cheese dinners, etc.—may be small and inexpensive, but they lessen the strain of life on the field and provide a boost for the entire missionary family.

One Wycliffe missionary family received a Christmas box from their home church through a particularly thoughtful friend. The church had placed a notice in their Sunday bulletin to facilitate the gift giving, which included Christmas ornaments and notes from a wide circle of their friends.

Commendation

Another scriptural principle linked to missionaries being "sent" is that of commendation: "Let other people praise you—even strangers; never do it yourself" (Prov. 27:2, Good News). "For it is not the one who commends himself who is approved, but the one whom the Lord commends" (2 Cor. 10:18). "Every matter must be established by the testimony of two or three witnesses" (2 Cor. 13:1).

It can be a dilemma for us to describe our upcoming or present missionary service, often putting us in the awkward position of "commending" ourselves. We may feel as though we must sell ourselves and our worthiness to receive support. It is not only awkward for us but also for our friends. We are instead to give the "word of our testimony," which gives glory to God, not to ourselves. A person who speaks on his own authority is trying to gain glory for himself. "...But he who wants glory for the one who sent him is honest, and there is nothing false in him" (John 7:18, Good News).

We need others who know us, trust us, and love us to endorse and commend us. Without this, we are open to criticism and suspicion. If others don't endorse us, people may question our credibility. Those who commend us also help shoulder the responsibility of seeing our ministry launched.

Ask the Lord to point out someone who might become your advocate in support raising. Your pastor and church leaders are an obvious place to begin. Having their public commendation will set the foundation for others to believe in you and your ministry. They may even ask, from the pulpit, for the congregation to pray about supporting you, both financially and through prayer. They can do this not with a manipulative, pressured presentation but with one of loving commendation and invitation to partnership in ministry.

An excellent example involves a couple whose home church is in Texas. After they had served with a missionary organization for almost two years, the wife was able to visit the church and was interviewed by their pastor in front of the adult congregation of about four hundred people. The pastor endorsed their ministry from the pulpit and invited the congregation to pray about supporting them monthly or with onetime gifts. He included a response device in the bulletin and encouraged people to realize that no gift was too small. As a result sixty-five people responded with approximately $600 in support pledged monthly plus $500 in onetime gifts. This provided a much-needed boost in meeting their needs.

Individual friends can also be strong advocates for your ministry. They may want to host dinner or dessert get-togethers for you, speak to others on your behalf, etc. They could potentially raise support for you, in much the same way as the pastor in Texas. Credibility and integrity are exhibited when someone else—a trustworthy and respected person—endorses your ministry and assists you in establishing a support team.

At the least, have a letter of reference as your means of others' commending you. If possible, obtain letters from both your pastor and the mission agency you are joining. A positive letter of endorsement is more valuable than much of what you could say. You can't brag about your abilities and calling. Others can.

I've written several letters of commendation and thanks on behalf of others, including my assistant, Mary. Once I sent a letter to fifty people on her behalf, personally addressing each one. I thanked them for their role in her life and presented several prayer requests, including her financial needs. I asked them to ask the Lord about their involvement and enclosed a response slip and envelope. Surprisingly, over half of the people receiving letters responded over a four-month period. As a result, her monthly financial support doubled, the number of monthly supporters also doubled, and she received nearly $1,500 in onetime gifts. In addition, a prayer group committed to pray for her regularly.

Another long-term missionary family who had struggled for many years with inadequate support experienced a similar response after letters of commendation and thanks were sent by their boss. As a result, an almost overwhelming flood of responses came to this family. Large onetime gifts, as well as new monthly supporters, resulted. They were seeing their "season of want" turned into "a season of plenty." Sending and commending are both acts of generosity by those taking part, resulting from our generosity toward them. It is a living example of 2 Cor. 8:14, "...in turn their plenty will supply what you need."

Summary

Practical ideas for friend raising, and the amazing, creative power of the Holy Spirit working within you, should give you plenty to begin with! Whether through visits, letters, your church's blessing, or surprising innovative avenues, friend raising is an adventure in interdependence. With strong dependence on God and strong interdependence with His people, a long-term ministry team forms, with those involved receiving blessing. Expect God to surprise you with His delightful gifts through Himself and others!

The following chapter identifies the more common pitfalls. Beware of the hurdles that may cause you to trip. Read with caution and alertness. You may discover areas that could cause future damage if not cared for in the present.

A friend does not cringe
at the drop of a flaw, but
picks up the shards carefully,
scrutinizing each
to better mend the whole.

— 7

HIDDEN
HINDRANCES

*"So, if you think you are standing firm, be careful that
you don't fall! No temptation has seized you except what is
common to man. And God is faithful; he will not let you
be tempted beyond what you can bear. But when you are
tempted, he will also provide a way out so that you can
stand up under it." (1 Cor. 10:12–13)*

SECURE IN OUR CALLING, WE MAY APPROACH SUPPORT
raising with many of the right concepts of friendship, generosity, communication, and prayer, yet still not experience
God's blessings on our support. There may be nasty hindrances hiding in a corner, overlooked by our searching eyes.
We must cry out, "Search me, O God, and know my heart;
test me and know my anxious thoughts. See if there is any
offensive way in me, and lead me in the way everlasting"
(Ps. 139:23–24).

Hidden hindrances are fundamentally bad attitudes manifesting themselves in unchristian behavior. They must be
recognized and dealt with if we are to overcome them.

Hindrance #1: Manipulation

Friends were planning to attend a special event. Without thinking, I said, "I wish I could afford to go." I heard my heart implying, *If only they gave to me, I could go too!* I manipulated them; I set them up to feel sorry for Poor Missionary Betty and her miserable life of want. I was disgusted with myself! Manipulation kills generosity: money may change hands, but the grace of giving has fled.

Before I understood the principles of generosity and giving and receiving, I would putt-putt to church, adding a few miles to the two hundred thousand already on my "missionary style" twenty-year-old VW Bug, and park among the shiny new cars, mentally calculating their probable purchase prices and monthly payments. Entering the church, I would scan the fancy clothes and jewelry, guessing costs and engaging my imagination in "judgmentship." Needy Betty wanted some too! When I talked to my friends, I feared they could see dollar signs clicking up like slot machine sour grapes in my eyes!

God was aware of the covetousness eating away inside of me. I was aware—and I was pretty certain others were aware of it too. In my time of need, I walked in desperation, clinging to people rather than to God. Slowly and gently, He began to change me.

A missionary may write, "I may have to leave the mission field. My finances are gone. If I don't hear from you soon, I'll have to quit!" This has manipulation written all over it. We've all experienced offerings tainted with manipulation. We've also experienced the Holy Spirit's generosity moving through an audience, motivating us to give. It's a joyous event that blesses both giver and receiver.

Corrie ten Boom lived with strong acknowledgment that God was her source of strength, not those who gave money. She made an indelible impression on me once after she gave a moving message in an auditorium of thousands of Christians. There was great potential for a large offering. But she stunned us before the offering was taken by saying, "I'd rather have a dollar which the Lord directs you to give, than a thousand which He hasn't!"

I thought, *Wow! Isn't that right?!*

Corrie only wanted what God told people to give, nothing more, nothing less. Her ministry was dependent upon Him, not us.

Wouldn't we rather have the dollar the Lord sends our way than the thousand He doesn't? Or are we so desperate that we will take *any* money, whether it comes from His hand or not? We can trust in *His* provision but not something of our own making. That requires the adventurous walk of faith on which God wants to lead us.

When we are needy, whether emotionally, financially, or physically, our weaknesses are glaring. Stripped of comfort and security, our frail humanity is exposed and often manifests itself in manipulation, coercion, or pressure.

People whose needs are not being met can become clinging, clawing, greedy, and ugly. Desperation can devastate the lives of Christians—even of missionaries—so that they are tempted to grab others by the neck and demand help: "You've got the money! I see your nice clothes, your cars, your homes! You could support me with very little of what you spend on yourself!"

On the other hand, desperation in seasons of want—as in Philippians 4—is gloriously redeemed when it turns us to God, who is "our glory and the lifter of our heads." J. Hudson Taylor, founder of China Inland Mission, wrote, "As a rule, prayer is answered and funds come in, but if we are kept waiting, the spiritual blessing that is the outcome is far more precious than exemption from the trial."[1]

Beware of the warning symptoms of "attitude disease": a desire to manipulate, coerce, and pressure! We must allow the Holy Spirit to sensitize us to these traits in ourselves.

It is even possible to develop a support base with skillful application of these attitude-disease traits. Many Christian and non-Christian groups have used manipulation and pressure with apparent success. However, the long-term benefits from such support sour when they are based on man's devices of guilt or obligation or pressure. But when we use God's principles, the fruit and mutual benefits increase and endure.

When we retain lordship over our funding and support raising, we operate with nonliberating pressure. When Jesus Christ is truly Lord over our support raising, as well as over all other aspects of our lives, we operate in liberating generosity.

We need to encourage potential supporters to give themselves first to the Lord, then to us *if* He so directs. If God does *not* so direct, that will not affect our relationship, which is founded on friendship and not on money anyway. *Relationship based on money is bondage.* Even a sizable one-time gift of money should not be an invitation to a barrage of fund-raising appeals!

Once I arranged a fund-raising banquet for a Christian ministry, using all the rules I had learned at a fund-raising seminar. We placed soft, burgundy leather Bibles embossed in gold by each place setting for anyone who either gave a one-time gift of $250 or pledged $20 per month for the next twelve months. The Bibles were almost screaming, "Touch me! Flip my pages! Give the money! Take me home!" From the 350 people who attended, we raised over $20,000, far exceeding the average success of a first-time fund-raising banquet.

At church the following Sunday morning, one of my personal supporters shoved the Bible back into my hands and said, "I want my money back. I gave the other night not because I wanted to but because I was pressured to."

I was practically speechless. I accepted the Bible, apologized, and promised to return his check. At the same time, I learned one of the most significant lessons I've ever learned about fund raising: instead of operating on God's principle of generosity—giving and receiving—I had operated on the world's principle of merchandising—buying and selling. We sold Bibles that night! God's principle of generosity is an act of love, never manipulation or pressure or enticement. Because obtaining the new Bibles was the primary enticement for giving that night, we had preempted any expression of generosity. We were in the Bible-selling mode—one Bible for $250!

I wonder how much of the $20,000 that night was like Corrie ten Boom's dollar that God directed. And I wonder how much was due to man's pressure to give. If we hadn't traded those Bibles, it would have been a wonderful banquet. That single element stained the whole evening.

Once we realized the error, we were repentant. We quickly changed our ways and sent the rest of the Bibles as surprise thank-you gifts to other donors who had made significant contributions or who had been supporters for a long time. We received wonderful love notes in return. Generosity gives freely and receives freely.

Both the capstone and the bottom line of Philippians 4:10–20 is "Give glory to God!" He is our source, not only of the resources from which we give but even of our own desire to be generous and thereby reflective of His character. Manipulation defames His character. We must be transformed into the image of Christ, the One who modeled grace, truth, and freedom but never manipulation.

Hindrance #2: Spiritual Attack from the Enemy[2]

"For our struggle is not against flesh and blood, but against the rulers, against the authorities, against the powers of this dark world and against the spiritual forces of evil in the heavenly realms" (Eph. 6:12).

Satan's principalities and powers of darkness do not want Christians to succeed, especially missionaries who carry the light of the gospel into the world. They do not want our needs to be met. They hinder us by inflicting frustration, confusion, and discouragement whenever and wherever possible. Sometimes their opposition is all that stands in the way. Lack of finances is one way in which Satan picks off missionaries. They give up. They get tired of fighting the fight and struggling in a lifestyle of want—until they have no fight left.

Described in three of the four gospels, Jesus' first significant activity after His baptism by John the Baptist was being sent by the Spirit to the desert to confront Satan. As Jesus led, so should we follow. One of our first tasks is to lay a spiritual foundation in our ministry through spiritual warfare. We should not become preoccupied with Satan, yet we should also not be unaware and caught off guard.

Satan is described in Scripture as the accuser of the brethren, a murderer, liar, thief, and deceiver. We can expect these traits to emanate from the Enemy's camp.

Let's look at Jesus' model in confronting Satan and his attacks. In the desert Satan tempted Jesus in three categories: lust of the flesh through food, lust of the eyes through authority over the kingdoms of the earth, and pride of life through testing God's ability to save Him. In each case, Satan presented a counterfeit offer, one that surprisingly included even God's own Word. Satan also began each temptation by questioning Jesus' identity, saying, "*If* you are the Son of God...." We, too, should be prepared for attacks

on our identity and calling in ministry. The Enemy's taunts—
"Who do you think you are?!"—must not be allowed to paralyze us nor prod us to ungodly action. We need to focus on who God is, not on who we are. Our response, like Jesus', must be grounded in God's perspective, the Word of God. Jesus countered each offer with the clear Word of God, not twisted as Satan had used it but clear, applicable, and full of truth.

Jesus had three responses to Satan's tempting offers:

- He spoke the applicable Word of God,
- He resisted the Enemy, and
- He commanded him to flee.

We, empowered by Him who has overcome the Enemy, are also called to respond likewise.

The first temptation was aimed at Jesus' greatest felt need—food for His physical needs. When we get hungry or there's not enough for our physical needs (shoes for the kids, money for paying utilities, etc.), we become vulnerable to Satan's attack. Immediately, he begins lying to us—"You really made a mistake this time. God didn't *really* call you. Wouldn't you rather have your old job back? Think of your kids!" Satan often tempts us by offering less than God's best to meet our present physical needs. He attacks us at our place of weakness. When we are desperate with unmet needs, we are vulnerable to counterfeit solutions.

Satan's other two tempting offers to Jesus had to do with power, prestige, and questioning God's character. We, too, can expect temptations in these areas.

I remember once when the Lord clearly spoke to me about finishing up my work with one ministry to begin with another. Almost immediately I was offered an attractive high-level position with a ministry other than the one to which God was leading me. It was very tempting! It strongly appealed to my pride and presented an attractive offer of power and prestige. Yet I came back to God's word to me and knew I would be disobedient to Him if I accepted. Once convinced of God's truth, I aimed my life toward that to which God had called me, putting on blinders to tempting offers.

Paul identifies truth in Ephesians 6:14 as one of our strongest weapons in spiritual warfare, providing protection against Satan's lying nature. Jesus describes Satan in John 8:44: "He was a murderer from the beginning, not holding to the truth, for there is no truth in him. When he lies, he speaks his native language, for he is a liar and the father of lies." We can expect lies and misrepresentations of the truth from the Enemy. He twists facts and presents lies to us and to others. Therefore, truth is central. It includes personal assurance of our calling as well as promises in Scripture, many of which are listed in chapter 5.

The Enemy may fill our minds with doubts. We may question our friends' concern for us when we don't hear from them or support drops off. We may also experience broken relationships purely due to friends' misunderstanding of what God is calling us to—again, missing aspects of truth. When we walk in the truth, we can see the Enemy's hands tied, relationships restored, and God's promises for us fulfilled.

Righteousness is the second element of our spiritual armor, described in Ephesians 6. We may be walking in truth but not in righteousness or godliness—and walk right back into the Enemy's camp.

Faith is another key part of our warfare tools. Our faith in God's calling and His promises to us becomes our shield of protection during times of spiritual attack. Fiery darts otherwise may find a tinder box awaiting the destructive flame.

The only offensive weapon that Paul describes is the Word of God. Remember this key in times of attack, especially in areas of the mind. Many of the attacks from Satan come in the form of thoughts and doubts. With the Word of

God as our offensive weapon, we can slice through the lies dropped into our minds.

Paul's final directive in Ephesians 6:18 is to "...pray in the Spirit on all occasions with all kinds of prayers and requests...." Without utter dependence upon God to answer our prayers and without the Spirit's leading us in prayer, we are unable to walk in truth, righteousness, and peace. We are empowered by the Spirit: "...another Counselor to be with you forever—the Spirit of truth....he lives with you and will be in you" (John 14:16–17).

A strong admonition to spiritual warfare is found in Revelation 12:11: "They overcame him [the accuser of the brethren] by the blood of the Lamb and by the word of their testimony; they did not love their lives so much as to shrink from death." This scripture seems to show that our strength in spiritual warfare is based on three things:

- Jesus' victory on the Cross, and His victory over Satan, is the primary basis for our personal victory. Jesus said, "...the ruler of this world is coming. He has no power over me" (John 14:30, Good News).
- The word of our testimony of God's faithfulness in provision, relationships, and love enables us to boldly speak God's truth in overcoming Satan.
- Walking in freedom from the fear of death and being willing to obey God at any cost snatches the element of fear out of Satan's hands. He loves to issue fear-filled and life-threatening taunts, especially as we venture into missionary service.

One final comment on spiritual warfare, with application to finances: generosity itself is spiritual warfare against greed and materialism, attacking Satan's stronghold over money. As we are generous with those God brings into our lives, God ignites generosity in others who may be restricted by Satan's ploys.

However, as we cling to our resources, we may fall prey to the Enemy's lies, leading us to unbelief and defeat. With spiritual discernment, we can expose and break Satan's influence by joining together with other believers and engaging in spiritual battle. "May God arise, may his enemies be scattered; may his foes flee before him" (Ps. 68:1).

Hindrance #3: Neglected Commitments

Debts, pledges, and commitments are serious business. Covenants and commitments are precious in God's estimation. Ecclesiastes 5:5 (Good News) warns, "Better not to promise at all than to make a promise and not keep it." Numbers 30:1–2: "This is what the LORD commands: When a man makes a vow to the LORD or takes an oath to obligate himself by a pledge, he must not break his word but must do everything he said."

Serious consequences, either positive or negative, result when commitments are either kept or broken. "…let your 'Yes' be 'Yes,' and your 'No,' 'No'; anything beyond this comes from the evil one" (Matt. 5:37).

Bible teacher Earl Pitts stresses that improperly handled debt can restrict our finances. When we have not lived up to our covenants and promises, or have not acknowledged our debts and "stood up to them," whether by fifty cents a month or a hundred dollars a month, Satan may have a foothold in our finances.

Many people today are burdened by debt and held back from leaving for the mission field. Recently I received an e-mail saying, "I desire to be a missionary in Manila, Philippines. My wife is from Quezon City, just outside of Manila…you might ask yourself why haven't I 'taken the plunge'? I've asked myself the same question and answered it as follows: debt. Credit card debt and student loan debt. It should take about three years to 'naturally' pay off my creditors, but I'm not going to rule out the merciful hand of God to help me out. I do need His help!...I want to go to the Philippines 'yesterday' but I can't drag my debt with me." As this young man expressed, his debt was entangling him. Be warned: each of us is to be wary of debt's gripping tentacles, seeing debt as an enemy, not a friend. Many of us are too comfortable with debt as a constant companion.

I, too, have personal experience with the challenge of neglected commitments. During my stint at YWAM's Discipleship Training School in January 1985, I wanted to rise up in generosity and watch God do new things in my life regarding finances. So I went forward and made the biggest faith promise of my life. However, several months passed, and I had paid only a portion of it.

Then in December of 1985, at YWAM's twenty-fifth anniversary celebration, my heart cried, "Take me to new heights, Lord! Take me to where You live in generosity, in giving, in freedom of money!" That's when I made an even bigger faith promise—four times as large as the first!

Then I settled down to wait for the lump sum to drop into my lap within the time frame of my pledge. I would win a contest, inherit a fortune, or be surprised in some other way. It would be the exact amount needed, and I would know it was God's precise provision for me to fulfill my pledges.

What a testimony I would have, giving all the glory, of course, to God!

The due date came and went. I still did not have the money. I had failed God, myself, and YWAM. And I crawled under the blanket of failure.

Then I heard Earl Pitts say, "If you are in debt, you have several options: If it was a pledge which you feel was made in error, you may ask to be forgiven and released from the pledge. If you are forgiven, then debt has no more influence either on you or on the other person (or organization). You do not owe the money; you are not in debt; you are free, and the other party is free as well.

"Second option: ask God what amount you should trust Him for each month to start standing up to your debt. Then watch Him meet you in provision toward that debt."

I sensed I was to go for the second option and trust God for $100 a month. I began writing out the checks. Some months I was able to give $300 and $400, and I soon paid all the pledges in full. The money bought windows for the GO (Global Outreach) Center at YWAM's university campus in Kona, Hawaii, symbolic to me of windows to God's beauty, windows to the nations of the world. Only after standing up to my debt could I rightly respond. As I confronted my neglected commitment, God met me with His fullness.

I once shared a meal with a struggling missionary who didn't have enough support to pay her rent. Discouraged by living expenses, old loans, and a pledge to her home church, she was $3,000 in debt and had stopped tithing. As I listened to her, the Holy Spirit convicted me about my own failure to tithe on an inheritance. Instead I had invested the money with no way to get at it without penalty.

God prompted me to confess it to her, then He gave me the crazy, wonderful idea to give one-tenth of my tithe to her! I had enough cash on hand to do that. Technically speaking, I had still not fully tithed, but I soon was able to complete my tithe when the investment was free.

It helped us both: it encouraged her and enabled me to stand up to the debt I had been numb to until the Holy Spirit convicted me. The next week, due to my gift plus her own resources, she was able to fly home to meet with supporters and spend time with family and friends. She stood up to her debts, walked in God's principles, and had one-third of her debts forgiven by both church and creditors. God again had redeemed a sin in my life and, at the same time, aided someone else precious in His sight. But, as Paul asks in Romans 6:1, "Shall we go on sinning so that grace may increase?" No! We are called to integrity, to stand up to our debts and to handle well what we have, including both possessions and commitments.

The principle of standing up to debt applies also to the pledges of others to us. When donors commit to us, they've made a contract, an ethical vow. If that vow is broken, it affects not only us but them as well. Should we, like Paul, say, "Now finish the work, so that your eager willingness...may be matched by your completion..." (2 Cor. 8:11)? Here we need discernment from the Lord; should we be silent and not confront, or lovingly call into account (which is often a way of blessing for supporters)?

Improperly handled debts reap negative consequences for both parties. It is important to maintain the friendship and help in their struggles, maybe with teaching tapes on finances or a note saying something like, "Are you unable to fulfill your pledge or to support me any longer? If that's the case, just let me know so I can plan accordingly."

Allow them to back out gracefully. Express a spirit of generosity and forgiveness.

Many of us are so afraid to speak the truth in love that we don't speak the truth at all. Once, a third of my support team neglected to send their pledged support for several months, and I had no idea why. Prompted by the Lord to write them, for their benefit as well as mine, I prayed over the letter, then ran it by a trusted friend to test its integrity before mailing it out. Would it cause disaster or not?

In the letter, I admitted my presumption upon our relationship, having assumed they would always be there for me.

Yet I had not been concerned and praying for them as I should. I asked for forgiveness, then explained the situation and told of my struggle with whether to be quiet or open and honest. I wrote:

> After spending time getting counsel from the Lord, I felt that both were appropriate, that being quiet about my poor attitudes was important, yet being honest with the struggle is only fair to you. We've made a commitment to one another, and honesty is part of that commitment. Just let me know. For those of you who have had problems, please know that I want to understand your situation. I'd much rather you'd inform me of why you're unable to send the support, so that I can cinch my belt tighter or raise more support. I don't want you to feel guilty, yet without knowing why you are unable to send in your support, I'm caught short of an adequate living allowance check each month (although God has always made things work out).

I put no undue dependence on them, yet I did give them a place in my life. I urged them just to be honest with me and to fulfill our covenant with one another. The response was interesting. I didn't lose a single supporter, but neither did I receive one letter or word in response to mine. My support, however, went back up to normal. Once again, giving bold attention to neglected commitments had a positive result. Ignoring it would have allowed the neglect to remain, causing damage to all involved.

A tremendous tool to help keep us out of debt and handling our commitments rightly is a budget. With prayerful planning, we can set financial guidelines to enable us to be good stewards. A helpful tool, *God's Managers*, is described in the "Where to Go for More Help" section at the back.

Hindrance #4: Poverty Mentality

"...Let me be neither rich nor poor. So give me only as much food as I need. If I have more, I might say that I do not need you. But if I am poor, I might steal and bring disgrace on my God" (Prov. 30:8–9, Good News).

All of us experience seasons of plenty and seasons of lack. Both can be right and good. God's Word gives place for both but not usually to a life of extreme poverty, except in lifestyles like Mother Teresa's.

If we are caught in a lifestyle, rather than a season, of want, we need to ask God for keys to freedom from a poverty mentality that restricts finances, wears us down, and lures us into despair, greed, selfishness, and unbelief. The longer we allow a poverty mentality to operate in our lives, the more it permeates our hearts and thoughts. It can actually lead to a love of money as our funds begin controlling our lives and taking the place of the Lord in decision making. We grab on to money for dear life, rather than clinging to the One who *gave* us dear life! We walk in independence, apart from God and His ways. It can lead quickly to destruction and further poverty.

Two common problems emerge almost every time I meet with full-time Christian workers who are desperately struggling with support: they are usually not tithing—not because they don't understand or believe in tithing but because they feel they can't afford to tithe and usually have little experience with it. They are also usually in debt.

Lack of generosity, failure to tithe, mismanaging finances that God has entrusted to us, and lying down under some kind of debt or unbelief can introduce a spirit of poverty into our lives. We forget the fish and loaves and God's ability to take the little we have and multiply it to meet our needs. We're out of touch with that aspect of God's character. This could stem from ignorance but leads to unbelief, which is sin.

Poverty says, "Scrounge for your clothes. You don't need decent shoes. Expect a junker car. You can't afford to go on a ministry trip. Don't even consider it!" It's true that sometimes God asks us to make sacrifices, but we're not paupers or beggars. That isn't to be our attitude—to expect the least.

When I began working with Youth With A Mission, I needed a car. Wanting to rightly handle the finances that God entrusted to me, I told my supporters, "I'm going to go in with some others on a junker car because I only need basic transportation."

But I sensed God saying, "No, you're not going to buy a junker car. I want to give you a good one."

So I waited. A couple of months later, my mom gave me a sum of money, enough for a nice used Toyota Tercel and the insurance. Even when I test-drove it, I questioned God because it had an automatic rather than a manual transmission, which would have been more economical. I sensed a still, small Voice saying, "Many people will drive this car. You need an automatic." Sure enough, God's gift to me was also a gift to many others.

We forget that God never said to look to our resources to determine His will but to ask Him, "Father, what do You want me to do? Where next, and what steps do You want me to take to get there?"

He may say, "Go to Asia to attend a missions conference, to visit and encourage the missionaries…"

I have taken several trips to Asia requiring thousands of dollars. Before two of the trips, I wrote a newsletter explaining the trip I believed the Lord was directing me to take. I explained the purposes, my own excitement, the amount of money needed, and the timing. I also enclosed response slips and remittance envelopes.

For both trips, the amount of money that was sent in response to the letter was exactly what I needed! In both cases, I had projected more money than was needed, and God supplied only what I needed. I found out afterward how precise He had been.

After one of my trips to Asia, I sent small thank-you gifts. They were touches of Asia—small Chinese silk paintings, silk embroideries, and stamps from Asia. They only cost about one dollar each. I included a personal letter, asking my supporters of the trip to use the gift as a reminder to pray for Asia, where two-thirds of the world's people live, the majority of whom have never heard of Jesus. It was a project in which thirty-five people participated.

In my years of world travel in full-time Christian ministry, I have rarely had funds up front for a trip I had to pay for myself. First, knowing the trip is God's will, I book the tickets, then move forward, saying with each step, "OK, God, now what do I do?" In response to that prayer, I sometimes send out a newsletter to people who have been a part of my life, describing the purpose of the trip and the prayer requests, then watch God do the selecting. I start walking the walk of faith, not of sight.

When we walk by sight, intimidated by the lack of dollars in our wallets, we're walking in the spirit of poverty. Even when we believe for finances for a complete round-trip, but then leave certain basic needs unmet and scrimp on normal gift-giving, ice cream for our children, normal rest and relaxation, such as a movie, etc., we are basing God's will on our own resources—and a poverty attitude is taking control.

At its root, the poverty mentality says, "I can't afford it. My present resources limit me, and God is no bigger!" If this mentality is creeping into your life, kick it in the pants, knock it aside, wage spiritual warfare, and *repent!* Ask God for a new frame of reference.

Hindrance #5: Disobedience

Let me address this integral issue positively with a quote from the Word of God: "Happy are those who obey the Lord, who live by his commands" (Ps. 128:1, Good News). God blesses those who are called. He blesses those who hear Him and obey.

The contrary, however, can be a significant hindrance. If the Lord has clearly directed us to do something related to support raising and we have sidestepped it, we will reap a dead harvest. His blessing will be missing. We may become perplexed and discouraged. Perhaps it's related to a broken relationship, and we need to humble ourselves and ask for forgiveness. Or it may be failure to pay an outstanding debt. Or perhaps God already told us to write someone, letting our needs be known, but our pride was holding us back. Or perhaps we haven't said thank you to those who deserve it.

During different segments of working on this book, I sensed the Lord convicting me of being behind on my thank-you notes to supporters. With my busy schedule, I'd let them pile up. I sensed that I would not be free to work on the book until I had thanked my supporters. How could I write about God's principles, expecting His blessing on my work, when I wasn't being obedient to the very principles He'd taught me?

Others I know have not seen a breakthrough in their finances until they corrected a practical matter in their own lives (such as paying taxes, etc.). God is concerned with the details as well as the big areas.

It may be a simple act of obedience that is required to effect a significant change. What was the last thing the Lord made clear to you regarding your part in building your missionary support team? Are there other areas in your life about which God has specifically spoken to you and you haven't responded? Remember, "If I had ignored my sins, the Lord would not have listened to me. But God has indeed heard me; he has listened to my prayer" (Ps. 66:18–19, Good News). *We* do the possible…*He* does the impossible! Both are essential ingredients.

Hindrance #6: Ingratitude

One of the most overlooked aspects of support raising and building relationships is that of giving thanks, not only to the Lord, the giver of all good gifts, but also to one another.

Inadequate response for gifts is a common hindrance to relationship between missionaries and their supporters. Jesus commented in Luke 17:15–19 that only one of the ten lepers healed said thank you. It seems to be a common human trait! Missionaries fail to say thank you from either embarrassment at being constantly on the receiving end, forgetfulness, or being "too busy doing God's work." None of these is a legitimate excuse.

Whenever a thank you is in order but not expressed, there is a literal break in relationship, whether with God or with friends. God's principles require gratitude and its free expression. This failure alone could be the chief cause of diminishing support. A gift, whether small or large, deserves and requires a thank you.

"Bad fruit" results from the failure to give thanks. For example, one church I know of drops missionaries from the budget if they don't hear from them. Donors often discontinue support to those who do not respond with thanks. Aside from hearing that the gift was received, they have the right to know how the money was spent and what the prayer needs are. If donors do not receive an appropriate thank you, they may feel used or taken for granted. The importance of acknowledging a gift and expressing gratitude cannot be overemphasized. Communicating appreciation is a primary way of nurturing supporters, and it needs special priority. We cannot expect God to thank them for us.

Shame or embarrassment show a lack of understanding that receiving a gift is an honorable thing; it indicates that independence is operating rather than *inter*dependence. It is right to say, "Thank you. It's wonderful being knit together through your gift. I appreciate your sensitivity to the Lord and caring enough to send support at an especially critical time."

Letting them know that *they heard from God* is an act of generosity on our part. People are often uncertain about hearing from God when they really do! For us to confirm that they responded to the Holy Spirit in miraculous timing encourages them, thrills their spirits, and makes them rise up and say, "If I heard Him once, I can hear Him again. I wonder if He'll tell me again to write a check, or if I should take flowers to this friend, or if I should phone so-and-so?"

A single word of appreciation, whether by postcard, a brief note, or a phone call can change a life. We need to be gracious, and we need to be quick.

Another hindering aspect of ingratitude can be our negative response to others' ingratitude when we have sent or given gifts to them. If we in any way break relationship with them or fail to continue pursuing them in spite of their response, we respond with less than God's highest. Oswald Chambers once wrote, "[Jesus] never hurried through certain villages where He was persecuted, or lingered in others where He was blessed. Neither gratitude nor ingratitude turned our Lord one hair's breadth away from His purpose to go up to Jerusalem....The same things will happen to us on our way to our Jerusalem. There will be the works of God manifested through us, people will get blessed, and one or two will show gratitude and the rest will show gross ingratitude, but nothing must deflect us from going up to our Jerusalem."[3]

Hindrance #7: Lack of Integrity

How we handle the resources God entrusts to us often determines how He continues to do so. The parable of the talents concludes:

"Well done, good and faithful servant! You have been faithful with a few things; I will put you in charge of many things. Come and share your master's happiness!" (Matt. 25:21).

More Scripture verses touch on money management than on nearly any other subject, many declaring the consequences of both godly and ungodly management of funds. Biblically stated, financial management is stewardship. Our integrity and holiness in handling support funds will be seen by the world and is to be continually tested.

One Christian fund-raising speaker opened his session with the following challenge, "You who are handling corporate finances and fund-raising, beware! You are handling explosives!" Fund-raising activities can be couched in either goodness or greed.

We are to set the pace for the world in integrity. As Proverbs 11:3 states, "The integrity of the upright guides them...." Money is a pivotal issue that God uses in our lives to teach us many principles. How we manage money reflects our heart, our values, our character, and how we live our lives. The test of our integrity goes down to the penny, even to a postage stamp. God calls us to be clean and pure in the small things, so we will be faithful and true in the big things, scrupulous in the thousands and millions.

As shown in 2 Corinthians 8:17–22, Paul took the whole administration of the money for the churches seriously enough to send at least two men, Titus and an unnamed brother, to help. He wrote that he wanted to be above reproach in the administration of those funds. "We want to avoid any criticism of the way we administer this liberal gift. For we are taking pains to do what is right, not only in the eyes of the Lord but also in the eyes of men." In other words, Paul considered this matter so important that he himself and two others took responsibility for the administration of it.

Proverbs 10:9 warns, "The man of integrity walks securely, but he who takes crooked paths will be found out." The issue of integrity covers the following areas (and more):

- our financial accountability to supporters,
- careful accountability for all income and expenses,
- integrity in paying taxes (give unto Caesar what is Caesar's), even in the minutest matter,
- contacting donors if funds requested for a certain project exceed the need, and getting their permission to use the funds for other projects/needs,
- being completely honest in ministry-related reports (no exaggerating, omitting known important information, or presenting a more favorable picture than is true),
- giving an accurate picture of financial and prayer needs,
- being honest in our struggles and not wearing an "I'm the perfect Christian missionary" mask,
- allowing and asking trusted people in our lives to question us, test us, and "keep us clean," and
- in general, being honest and transparent with the Lord, ourselves, and with our supporters.

We are all called to be holy, set-apart people. Being reflective of our Lord Jesus, the spotless Lamb, we are called to an irreproachable lifestyle. We need continual sensitivity to the Holy Spirit to know what is clean and what is unclean. Our own judgments are often tainted by the world's opinion, which seems to become more impure and unscrupulous with every year.

Integrity in financial management for the missionary falls into several major categories:

- accountability for both income and expenses,
- tithing,
- generosity, and
- proper response to debt.

Falling short in any one of these areas may hinder support-raising efforts. I believe we're called to keep accurate, honest accounts. If we don't keep track of income and expenses, we are not being wise and cannot be sure whether we are tithing or being generous or cheating on taxes.

Tithing is a test of integrity, an act of faith. Since the tithe belongs to God, paying it is not an act of generosity but an act of simply paying what is owed. All Christians, whether in missionary "faith" lifestyles or in more traditional "paycheck" lifestyles, are to tithe regularly. Not to tithe is to literally steal from God's pocket. Malachi 3:8–10 says: "…you ask, 'How do we rob you?' In tithes and offerings. You are under a curse…because you are robbing me. Bring the whole tithe….Test me in this…."

In 1895, Wesley Chapel in Cincinnati encountered financial difficulties. In response, the congregation tried "suppers, festivals, lectures, stereopticon shows, subscriptions, and the whole round of man-made schemes and devices," according to layman William G. Roberts. However, when Roberts and others resorted to the idea of "storehouse tithing," the church turned around. Soon after, tithing was revived as a popular practice in churches in the United States.[4]

Interestingly enough, John Wesley, after whom the chapel was named, preached a great deal on money. He received one of the highest incomes in England at the time, yet he gave it away as quickly as he could. His practice matched his preaching. He preached that Christians should give away all income above that which was needed to take care of their family and creditors. He believed that as income increased, the standard of giving should increase but not the standard of living. One year his income was over £1400 but he kept only thirty.[5]

Jesus calls us to live beyond the Law in many areas of our lives; therefore, generosity is beyond the tithe of Old Testament law. No gift short of the tithe is a gift of generosity, no matter how generous we may feel at the time. It could be that we feel like we're tithing and giving generously, but without records we cannot know for a fact whether we are even being responsible. We could simply be putting coins in a bag with holes.

Our paperwork is a vital part of our ministry (see "Helps and Forms"). Without it we end up doing costly guesswork, diminishing our ministry. Integrity is required in all areas of our lives, whether in record-keeping, accountability, tithing, or in our communication to others. Are we reflecting our Lord Jesus' integrity in our affairs?

Hindrance #8: Spirit of Promotion

As mentioned in the "hindrance" related to integrity, we may be tempted to be less than completely honest in our ministry-related reports. We can tickle people's ears in a "spirit of promotion," or we can impart truth and life through "proclamation." One is couched in humility, the other in pride. One is empire building; the other is kingdom building.

I was once about to speak in a church about the ministry of YWAM. Prior to speaking, I was gripped by anxious thoughts. Few of the two hundred people present were famil-iar with YWAM, and I cried out to the Lord for help. I felt the Lord impressing two things on me: first, I was to care more about what He thought than what they thought; and second, I was to tell of YWAM's failures, not successes.

How radical! Who would have imagined that the best way to represent the ministry was to highlight its weak points and how the Lord had intervened? I followed the Lord's direction, and after the service fifty people stayed and asked for more stories of how God had met us in our weaknesses. That is the power of "proclamation," declaring what God has done in the midst of frail humanity. Proclamation presents an accurate picture, not embellishing but speaking the truth, warts and all.

If, however, we fall prey to a worldly spirit of promotion, we exalt our ministry and what we have done over and above what God has done. Motivated by selfish ambition or rooted in insecurity or fear of failure, promotion reflects our fallen nature and becomes an image-driven endeavor. We easily tend toward promoting things—whether ourselves, our loved ones, the mission we serve with, or our ministry. We desperately want to "put our best foot forward," and a spirit of promotion may take over, exalting that which we're pro-moting rather than God, distorting the truth, and potentially leading to deception and even "image worship" (idolatry).

Sadly, exaggeration is sometimes accepted in Christian circles. The contemporary phrase "evangelistically speaking" implies a stretched truth. Do we Christians have any busi-ness being conformed to the world and by the world through engaging in exaggeration? We are filled with the Holy Spirit, described in John 14:17 as the Spirit of truth, not exaggera-tion. We are called to be seekers of truth. "Every word of God is flawless....Do not add to his words, or he will rebuke you and prove you a liar....Keep falsehood and lies far from me" (Prov. 30:5–8).

The media has exposed numerous infractions of truth within the body of Christ. The U.S. television program *Prime Time* did an exposé in the 1990s on three televangelists caught up in exaggerated promotion. Sadly, as facts were uncovered, it became apparent that gross distortions and even lies had been used to impress the televangelists' viewers in order to raise funds. The "love of money" led the televangelists—and all of us—into dangerous territory.

Proclamation, ironically, is a far more powerful means of promotion. That Sunday morning I spoke in the church, YWAM's ministry was promoted in the best sense of the word. Yet it was through proclamation that it occurred. "If I must boast, I will boast of the things that show my weakness...so that Christ's power may rest on me....For when I am weak, then I am strong" (2 Cor. 11:30; 12:9–10). The fifty people who stayed on after church were starved for life-giving stories of human failure and God's redemption—GOOD NEWS! We hunger for Good News—God's news—describing God's power in the midst of our fallen humanity. (I'm not endorsing hanging out all our "dirty laundry." As in everything, we need to ask God for His wisdom in what to share, with whom, and when, regarding our failures and how He redeemed them.)

Being committed to proclamation doesn't mean that we can't describe what we have accomplished, but we do need to be very careful about the way in which we do so. Are we exalting people, events, or personalities? Or are we giving all glory to God?

Brennan Manning writes:

> These words [1 Peter 5:5–6] are both frightening and consoling. God resists, refuses, rejects the proud.

But He delivers Himself up, He gives Himself totally to the humble and the little....When my insecurities, low self-esteem, and negative self-image lead me to subtle boasting about my accomplishments, when I wax eloquent about the incomparable beauty and extraordinary unity of my marriage or the fantastic achievements of my children, when I try to impress others with the range of my knowledge and the depth of my prayer life, all the while giving lip service to the power of the Holy Spirit, I am directing your attention to myself and stealing from Jesus.

"Without me," Jesus said, "you can do nothing." The humble Christian echoes the cry of Mary in her Magnificat, "He has been mindful of the humble state of his servant....The Mighty One has done great things for me...." (Luke 1:48–49)[6]

Hindrance #9: Unforgiveness

Numerous occasions will arise requiring forgiveness. If, however, we are unable to forgive either ourselves or others when a wrong or failure occurs, we will enter a self-destructive cycle. Without forgiveness, we are broken people without any hope of healing. Our supporters and friends will no doubt disappoint us. We will no doubt disappoint ourselves, God, and others. The open door to the future is titled "forgiveness." "How good and pleasant it is when brothers live together in unity!...For there the LORD bestows his blessing, even life forevermore" (Ps. 133:1, 3).

Failing to hear from loved ones back home—from those friends who were the most likely to support us and write us but didn't—requires the healing balm of forgiveness and understanding. If we discontinue corresponding with people, whether by personal notes or newsletters, purely due to their lack of response, we will hurt both them and ourselves. *Only* stop contact if you feel the Lord's leading in this. A lack of response may be only a breakdown in communication. They may be praying for us and inspired by our letters but are simply poor letter writers.

One missionary couple told me they removed a number of people from their mailing list after a year of not hearing from them. The very next month they received support from several whom they had removed. They quickly learned only to remove people carefully, under the guidance of the Holy Spirit.

I am often discouraged by the lack of mail from supporters and other friends. Yet when I see people face to face, I am often surprised by many who comment that they are praying for me either daily or otherwise. What a loss if I were to drop communication with them based on perceived loss of interest!

Most of the world is made up of poor letter writers. If we fail to extend grace and mercy to others, we will fail to experience much of God's blessings. This failure also leads us back into enemy territory as described under Hindrance #2. Unforgiveness keeps us distant from others.

We receive this same grace, mercy, and forgiveness in ample measure from the Lord, and we must pass on that which we've received. "But if you do not forgive men their sins, your Father will not forgive your sins" (Matt. 6:15). We also find a powerful spiritual principle about forgiveness in John 20:23, "If you forgive anyone his sins, they are forgiven; if you do not forgive them, they are not forgiven."

Summary

These hidden hindrances will keep us from freely running the race: manipulation, spiritual attack, neglected commitments, poverty mentality, disobedience, ingratitude, lack of integrity, spirit of promotion, and unforgiveness. May the Lord grant us wisdom and strength as we walk in His ways!

Notes

1. *Christian History*, Vol. Vll, No. 3, Issue 19, p. 7.
2. For further instruction on spiritual warfare, I recommend *Spiritual Warfare for Every Christian: How to Live in Victory and Retake the Land* by Dean Sherman; see the "Where to Go for More Help" section at the back of this book.
3. Oswald Chambers, *My Utmost for His Highest*, p. 267.
4. *Christian History*, Vol. Vll, No. 3, Issue 19, p. 20.
5. ibid., p. 24.
6. Brennan Manning, *Lion and Lamb: The Relentless Tenderness of Jesus* (Old Tappan, New Jersey: Fleming H. Revell Company, 1986), p. 57.

—

The simplicity of friendship
is this:
that I know you are there
that somewhere on this crowded
planet you and I stand together,
if only in a moment of thought.
And for those moments and
what they bring to me,
the world is less empty.

—

− 8

WILL IT WORK IN TIMBUKTU?

DOES THE CONCEPT OF FRIEND RAISING, AS OPPOSED TO fund-raising, apply everywhere in the world, regardless of culture or economic situation? Yes, when based on scriptural principles rather than on methodologies (practices) alone.

Non-Western Christian missionaries have responded to friend-raising principles with comments such as, "I have heard many fund-raising teachings, but this is the first one that feels right in my spirit. This concept works in my culture; other methods do not."

Principles or Practices

Distinguishing principles from practices is the key, regardless of the culture or economic situation. That which is honestly based on Scripture is principle; that which otherwise prescribes "how-to" methods falls in the practices category. Scriptural principles, such as friend raising, generosity, communication, and prayer apply to everyone in all places at all times. Practices, however, need to be sensitively adapted to each culture.

Cling to scriptural principles but hold lightly to culturally based practices. Newsletters, response cards, and various presentations need to be reinterpreted within each cultural situation. In some parts of the world certain practices can be used, while in others they would be disastrous. Trust the Lord's counsel to discern what is appropriate in each situation.

As I taught the Guatemalan team of new missionaries mentioned in chapter 3, the power in God's Word on generosity birthed new faith within them. They saw potential within their own culture to which they had been blinded. Yes, they were poor, but that didn't limit God's truth from being applied. In the same way, the South American pastor who taught on giving (also mentioned in chapter 3) saw fruitful results of God's principles in action. God honors generosity when we operate according to His financial principles, and He adds to our wealth, no matter who we are. Paul describes a godly response in 2 Corinthians 8:1–2: "…we want you to know about the grace that God has given the Macedonian churches. Out of the most severe trial, their overflowing joy and their extreme poverty welled up in rich generosity."

God's principles are the same throughout the world, as shown in the following stories from other missions groups in other parts of the world.

From International Youth Missions

Rick "Ricardo" Johnson, Director of International Youth Missions, recalls the extreme generosity of the Yanomamo village of Coshilowateli, part of an Amazon jungle tribe in Venezuela. When the extreme plight of poor Mexicans living in the dumps of Tijuana was described to the impoverished Yanomamo Christians, they pleaded, "Oh, Ricardo, bring all the Dump People here to live. We will take care of them." When Rick explained the impossibility of doing so, the Yanomamos took a sacrificial offering among themselves (about ten U.S. dollars) for food for the starving people in the Dumpteli (Dump Village). Rick commented, "I learned a great lesson on giving from these brothers....I had to note that these Indians lack in all the theological training that we regard so highly here in our churches, but they easily latched on to God's desire to love and serve the poor. These Amazon tribal people still send money to help the poor living in the Tijuana Dump today. It is interesting to see how many times those who have so little give so much."

From Miracle Centre Church of God Mission in Nigeria

[Benson Idahosa] had always taught his people to give....In a nation where much of the population finds it difficult to scrape together enough food to stay alive, not many preachers deliver sermons on giving, but Benson did. A favorite text was Proverbs 11:24 (KJV): "There is that scattereth, and yet increaseth; and there is that withholdeth more than is meet, but it tendeth to poverty."

"When you scatter by giving this year, it shall yield return and multiply," he told his people. "But if you withhold it, it will tend you to poverty. Therefore, scatter and it shall increase, for multiplication brings the glory of God. If you identify your money with His own money, God will multiply it for you.... If you give Him any kind of gift, it shall bring forth fruit of its own kind. No one ever beats God at giving. He is a God of multiplication. When you give anything to God, He returns it to you in abundance. There is no shortage in God." (Taken from Fire in His Bones, by Ruthanne Garlock, 1982, p. 149.)

The people responded and began to give. They gave for the building project, for evangelistic crusades, for literature production, for television outreach, and for the needs of their pastors. Financial help also came from other partners, but the people of Miracle Centre Church of God Mission gave sacrificially. And the law of sowing and reaping worked, just as their pastor promised it would.

From Myanmar (formerly Burma)

In Myanmar tribal Christians set rice aside daily in order to finance their own frontier missionaries to neighboring tribes and beyond. As each mother prepared meals for her family, she set aside a handful of rice in a special container and prayed for her church's missionaries. Individually they were unable to give money, but each family gave rice, which was sold to support missionaries to unreached people groups in order to see God's kingdom expand.

From the U.S. Center for World Mission

The Burmese custom sparked the U.S. Center for World Mission to develop an American counterpart through Frontier Fellowship. Loose change has been substituted for rice in the daily custom. Each person's loose change averages over $100 per year.

From Theodore Williams of India

Theodore Williams of India described how some missionaries in northeastern India are supported by impoverished believers who sell rice and eggs. He said, "The traditional pattern of sending a missionary forth with full support guaranteed is not the only divinely ordained pattern."[1]

From the Philippines

A Filipino missionary failed in raising her support when her initial method was a sales pitch. But then she felt urged by the Lord to approach people in a friend-sharing-with-friend attitude. As she shared honestly what God was calling her to do, she was able to be herself and offer others the freedom to respond, rather than pressure them to react. She quickly raised the needed support from her Filipino friends, some with considerable means, others with very little, but all within the framework of generosity.

As in this case, the primary source of support for any missionary should come from his or her own culture, from within the home church setting. It is there that strong friends within a solid missionary-sending framework exist. Ideally the home church should send out, support, love, and pray for its own.

A strong temptation exists, however, for workers from the poorer settings to reach out for funds from wealthier regions or nations. This may be proper in some situations to some degree, but beware of belittling God's principles of generosity in sowing and reaping, which are able to revolutionize the economic situation of even the poorest cultures.

These principles are often neglected and not taught because of disbelief. To give generously in the midst of abject poverty—when there is virtually nothing to give—makes no sense to the natural mind. But God's principles are true, regardless of the situation.

Despite their poverty, the Macedonians gave gifts for the Jews in Jerusalem, to the glory of God (Rom. 15:26). Despite poverty in the Philippines, the Filipino churches are also able to "well up in rich generosity." Each cultural setting is unique; yet all are made up of people who are created in the image of God and who have areas of receptivity to the principle of generosity.

Thailand

In Thailand, YWAM's Thai missionaries wrestled with the appropriate approach regarding missionary support. Due to the minuscule size of the Thai Christian church, coupled with a deeply rooted cultural resistance to supporting missionaries, the ideal of the church supporting its own was nearly impossible to realize. However, even as the church members watched their missionaries gain financial support from Christians outside of Thailand, the seeds of God's principles of interdependence, generosity in sowing and reaping, and missionary-sending were planted within their Thai churches.

Alternative vs. the Ideal

Creative alternatives may be necessary in difficult settings: tentmaking, for instance, may be the only point of entry for some countries. Teachers, health care workers, and others may have access to "closed" countries, earning income in the country in which they work. Although income is primarily provided through their work, these missionaries need the love, encouragement, and prayer support from friends and family at home as much as any other missionary. Too often, since income is guaranteed without support raising, there is no support team joined in ministry with the missionary. This need must not be neglected by the tentmaking missionary.

Tentmaking might also be a choice, not a requirement, for the missionary. If, however, tentmaking is chosen primarily for its financial benefits, to avoid support raising, I believe a loss will occur, both to the missionary and to his or her church back home.

It's a matter of calling. Are you called by God to be a tentmaker? Is it supportive of your ministry? Or is it hampering your ministry by consuming your time in work solely to provide income? I believe the benefits for a missionary in the lifestyle of interdependence far outweigh the benefits of predictable income. Don't let money dictate how you will spend your time on the field. Tentmaking may become a crutch that deters the missionary from fully pursuing his or her call. Know your call and stick closely to it.

Home churches need missionaries as much as missionaries need home churches. Many benefits are gained for both. Often home church members are refreshed by good news from the field, contrasted with most television or newspaper reports giving "Satan's news" describing murder, theft, and destruction.

Missionaries without a support system from their cultural roots often will be missionaries without any roots—floundering, unaccountable to anyone. While Christian workers from poorer nations may be tempted to look to believers in wealthier countries for financial support, it is important to recognize that supporters from another culture may become paternalistic. Therefore, we must dig into our own culture for our foundation of support and backup prayer. Doing so is necessary not only for our own well-being but also for that of our home community. When people at home partner with us, we learn God's ways together, growing in Him as we work for His kingdom.

Will it work in Timbuktu? Whether in rich cultures or poor, God's principles work! It is crucial for us to cling to God's Word and walk in His ways, being sensitive to appropriate cultural application.

Note

1. *Christianity Today*, Jan. 15, 1988. "Who Holds the Key to World Evangelization?" pp. 40–41.

—

Friendship is a place
where we go to grow —
where it is safe
to sprout wings,
and shed old skins,
and try our voices
in new, uncertain notes.

—

TESTIMONIES
THAT TALK!

THE FOLLOWING STORIES ILLUSTRATE MANY OF GOD'S principles in friend raising: interdependence, integrity, accountability, handling debt, communication with supporters, prayer with promises, Spirit-led personal invitations, financial stewardship, church accountability, and church sending. These missionaries have learned much about His ways and are led by the Lord in their friend-raising activities. I hope their stories are as encouraging to you as they are to me.

Mary Somers' Story

"Against all hope" was how the Lord encouraged me to stay in missions. I had been in missions for a couple of years and was plagued by heavy debts the whole time. Whenever I managed to wrestle my "balance due" to reflect smaller figures, a new medical crisis would obliterate my gains. This time I racked up more than $5,000 in medical bills in one week.

I had barely survived an asthma attack. The hospital nurses told me that I was clinically dead in the emergency room. I know I felt like something that had died. I was over four thousand miles from home, living by faith. With my legacy of ill health and other bills, I now owed $7,346.

I was almost overwhelmed, but I had friends. One of them put my problem in perspective by asking me, "What's the difference between $10,000 and $10 if you don't have any?" And they weren't just friends in talk; they helped with my bills. My coworkers paid a huge chunk of my medical debt.

But my debt stayed above $3,000 for the next two years. Ongoing medical expenses averaged $85 per month. I was receiving around $150 in committed monthly support, and I wasn't making it. Over the long haul I felt very much alone.

Interdependence was a hard thing for me to learn. It seemed easier to depend on some esoteric concept of "God will provide" than to get down to the nuts and bolts of its mechanics. I hated paying attention to all the paperwork—the accounts, the sitting down to pay bills every month, the letters to supporters, and the thank yous. It all seemed such a nuisance. I'd rather have ignored the details and people instead of learning God's ways through them—and I did ignore them.

The following two years, I attempted monthly payments and was only seasonally successful. I sometimes missed a month and occasionally two months. Then as my fourth year in missions approached, my "monthly" payments became "quarterly." I took advantage of my weak financial position. I felt I was untouchable. My attitude was, "They can't take anything from me but my word I'll pay, because all I have is worn sneakers." I would pay them, only I was no longer in a hurry to do it.

I thought those due dates didn't matter, but in reality every missed payment eroded my faith and ministry. Debt, not faith, began to define my existence. I couldn't hope beyond the sporadic godsend to forestall my next disaster. I never planned beyond the current month.

The longer that debt hung over me, the more I slid into survival mode. My resiliency lost its bounce. Life was so hand-to-mouth that perseverance became a lifestyle. I consumed every encouragement like a crazed nomad slaking thirst in a desert stream, and I was reluctant to leave those rare pools of refreshment for new ventures.

I got so weary of debts, of bare resources, of searching for answers! I eventually stopped writing my supporters, because I didn't feel I had anything good to share. I knew I should write them at least once a month. I even made some false starts at it, but after a few years, some of them rarely heard from me.

I sought solace from others in the same dilemma—I felt safe with them. No one had answers I hadn't already tried or considered. The only untried answer seemed to be leaving faith missions behind, but I was reluctant to go that way, because I felt God calling me to continue.

My motto became "don't give up," and I learned something I never understood before—courage is for daily living. I was barely holding on to my mission call—like a shipwrecked survivor clinging to flotsam with a white-knuckled grip.

Then I started transcribing tapes for this book. I began to realize that I didn't even know my own heart nor how far I had strayed from godly principles. That self-deception quickly dissipated as I tuned in—ears to earphones—to the facts. Hearing the principles over and over challenged my socks off. I transcribed more than fifteen tapes, sat in on the teaching more than a few times, proofed this book for errors, and ran off its many drafts. As if that weren't enough, I worked with the author daily and had to witness how she lived. Was God driving home a point or what?

The first idea to grab me was communication. I guess it was during the third or fourth tape I transcribed that I finally knew I couldn't listen to another word without writing a thank you to my supporters. Those were some awkward thank yous after such a long silence.

At first it was a disciplined chore, but then letters began to flow more easily. My support relationships came alive. As I faithfully wrote every month, God brought new supporters into my life. I now have some friends I've never met.

The second thing God pointed out was my checking account. I never balanced my checkbook. To me, it was just a bothersome detail. When I'd begin to get nervous about errors piling up, I'd cancel the account and open a new one somewhere else.

I had transcribed about seven tapes at that time, and I was cringing all the way through the sections on financial management. I started making jokes about "creative bookkeeping"—a kind of potion to soothe my throbbing conscience. It worked, too, until one day Betty overheard and called me on it. It was like "E. F. Hutton speaking." I later spent one long evening balancing my entire checking account. I came out about $40 ahead.

The third thing God pointed out was my "cookie fund"— that ration of disposable income that feeds half the zits across the face of the Western world. I've heard it said—and I fully believe it—that the last thing to submit to the kingdom of God is the cookie fund. (Cookies are a wonderful comfort for debt stress.)

Liquidation of my cookie fund was a radical change that required heavy pressure, provided unexpectedly by the IRS when I received a tax notice saying they were going to put a lien on me. Well, that touched the "untouchable." I got a nudge from the Lord that it was time I asked for advice from someone who knew a few things about support raising.

I humbled myself and asked for help. I gave Betty my accounts (at least I kept records) and asked her opinion. What I remember of our conversation—most of it was me talking, mind you—was her simple observation, "You're rationalizing."

Within thirty minutes of talking with Betty, I received news that two *new* people had committed to support me in prayer and finances. I knew right away that I needed to change my ways. I didn't have time to sort through all my rationalizations (I should live so long!). I seriously resumed *monthly* payments—with letters of apology—and choked the cookie fund. By that time, I had transcribed thirteen teaching tapes. Talk about "hearing the word" and "renewing the mind"!

It's been an ongoing process. New things come up from time to time. Once I was sitting in on Betty's teaching to take notes for the book. When she hit the high points of keeping pledges (how many times now?), all of a sudden I knew I had to write two more letters. The first was regarding a pledge I had broken over ten years before, and the second was about a fifteen-year-old stolen gym towel—much to my chagrin.

This time of intense transition has had its lighter moments. During one lean time, when the money wasn't there for me to meet those relentless due dates, God provided an interesting alternative. I called my doctor to let him know I couldn't make the full payment, but that I'd just sent such-and-such an amount. While we were on the phone, the billing clerk found an error in my bill. My new balance was exactly what I'd just put in the mail.

Hearing Betty's teaching over and over has been something of an adventure—its victories outmatch the twinges of guilt. My monster debt no longer looms so fearfully. Just before this book was published, I was able to put to rest two medical accounts that had haunted me for four solid years. Writing to supporters, addressing my monthly bills, and balancing my accounts have turned into times of restful assurance—I know those hours are well spent, pleasing to God.

My biggest payoff can't be measured. I now have a network of friends. I don't feel alone anymore. That was worth all the hours I spent working on this book.

Paul Hawkins' Story

Author's Note: Paul Hawkins, a seasoned YWAM missionary of nearly thirty years, is an inspiring model of raising support on the basis of relationships and faith. One afternoon he sat with me and "talked story" (as we say in Hawaii). The following is Paul's experience:

We have lived this life for more than twenty years. We started out with $250 a month support that decreased to $100 a month for a family of four. We existed for probably seven years knowing only where $100 a month was coming from. In that time our family traveled around the world three times. Our older son has been to thirty-six nations. Our younger son, at the age of fifteen, has been to twenty-four nations.

We have seen God's provision in many ways. We've never gone hungry. Whenever there's been a major financial or medical crisis, the money's always been there. Our children have never gone without shoes. We haven't had everything we wanted, but God has always been faithful to provide for us. Even when things were tight, Christmastimes were meaningful experiences. God has provided for us even in tight testing times.

A few years ago, I went to Loren Cunningham and said, "I'm concerned that everyone is writing letters asking for help. Who's going to 'faith it out'—just believe God and see it happen?"

He said to me, "It's just as miraculous when you pray and get some names to write letters to, and they write back saying, 'I've just been thinking about you,' as it is to have God speak to them directly."

I said, "All right. You got me." So I went home and prayed. Three people's names came to mind that I felt I was to write to, telling them our needs and asking for financial help.

The day after I mailed those letters, I received a phone message from a fellow I hadn't seen for ten years. He had moved to Hawaii and wanted to take me to lunch. Two days later we met. The first thing he asked was, "Paul, what are your needs?" It took me by surprise, but since I had just expressed my needs in a letter, I knew how to answer. I told him my needs, and he said, "I want to help you." However, he didn't say what that meant.

Then the Holy Spirit said to me, "You didn't tell Steve everything. What about the chair?" The doctor had recommended a special recliner massage chair for my wife, Peggy, to help her difficult back condition. It cost $750, but I didn't have the money for it.

So I said, "Excuse me, I haven't told you everything." I told him about Peggy's circumstances. He reached into his pocket, pulled out $750 cash, and said, "Go buy the chair."

During the following six months he lived in Hawaii, whenever I saw him [about three times], he handed me $500 or $1,000 cash. Then he said, "I think you need a new car. I think you need a new Honda." He didn't know that three years before, I'd had a desire that if I could buy a new car, I would like to buy a Honda. I never even told my wife. Today, I'm driving a new Honda.

Three months after the lunch date, I received a response to one of the three letters I had previously written. This friend said, "When I received your letter, I was so encouraged. I'd just been thinking about you, that I should send you some money. I'm sorry it took three months, but we've been busy with the new baby and the new house." Enclosed was a check for $3,500.

When you obey God, then He does other things miraculously. For example, I needed $2,000 to go to Manila for a conference. I immediately felt I was to write four people and ask for help for this particular project.

I wrote each of them. There was only one response in terms of financial support: "The minute I got your letter, I knew it was 'Yes,'" and they enclosed a check for $2,000. I then contacted all four people. I thanked each of them for obeying God, because the exact amount needed came in. [Author's note: Can you imagine receiving a thank-you note for not sending money?]

When we raised support for our son for King's Kids [a YWAM ministry], we prayed and felt we should write eleven people about raising the needed $1,000. The money came from five sources, not eleven, but we wrote all eleven people and said, "Thank you very much for your prayers and your obedience. The exact amount of money has come in. Everybody obeyed!" So, we thanked everybody.

I began to be stirred to raise support in a nation where I had been giving input for about ten years through my teaching ministry. I'd never felt led to raise support from people I had not worked with on an individual basis. But I felt the Lord told me to do it. I said to my wife, "I think I'm supposed to raise support from this nation, and I think it's through these seminars that I've been doing."

I wrote the seminar leader for permission to write people who had participated in the seminar, asking them for financial support. I sent the letter, and two days later I received a letter from him. It had been mailed two months previously and had accidentally gone to Asia before it came to me. He wrote, "What can I do to help you?"

I wrote him immediately, explaining that his letter had arrived after I had mailed my letter to him, and that I was so encouraged by his asking to help, since I was asking for his help. He wrote back and gave me permission to contact the seminar participants. Then we drafted letters in the language of the particular nation and sent them off with prayer. We included a letter that our International Director had drafted to help us raise support, our own cover letter, and a picture of our family.

The first response said, "When I read your letter, it took my breath away, because I've never received an answer from God so quickly in all my life before." She said God had impressed her to get involved in supporting missions worldwide, not just in her own nation. She also explained that she was coming into a new level of income, and had been asking God where it was to go. She said that my letter was the answer. She sent us a large gift plus made a substantial monthly commitment over the next year.

I've also taken Earl Pitts's teaching on budgeting and have sought the Lord about what my annual income is to be. I budget accordingly. I'm not to that [desired annual income] level yet, but that's what I'm working toward. God isn't going to drop it on us overnight. We couldn't handle all the relationships needed to be handled at one time. We have to prove our good stewardship of the relationships we now have before God will entrust more to us.

Once I was speaking in a school, and I said to my wife, "I think there are three couples we're to invite to lunch, all at the same time." Now, normally you don't do it that way. It puts people on the spot. But I felt we were to invite these three couples. I didn't even know if they knew one another. I invited the three couples. The eight of us sat down to lunch, and the conversation took off. It turned out that each couple had a relationship with the others in some context.

At the end of lunch, I expressed our needs to them, where we were financially, and asked them to consider helping us in prayer. One couple came back with $100 a month, the second couple with $50 a month, and the third couple with periodic gifts. That was almost three years ago. I've only done something similar one time since then, with one other couple.

Whenever I've felt an impulse regarding support raising, I try to test it rather than jump into it. That's the way I think God has called me. I'm committed to seeking God in detail in my lifestyle and decision making. When I write a letter and after months of delay get a response that specifically meets a need, I know it's a miraculous response from the Lord, even though I made the need known.

There are also times of faith testing with desert experiences. For example, the YWAM staff at our center was challenged to write letters asking for personal financial support. So my wife, Peggy, and I prayed and felt we should write to eleven friends who have never helped us financially. We got one response back, saying they would send us $15 a month. The day the first $15 check came, we got a letter from friends who had supported us for ten years at $20 a month and had never missed a month. They said, "We're sorry, but as of this month, we can't send you any more money." We lost $5 a month.

Another time, we were going on a long trip, so we made arrangements to visit our supporters on the mainland. After that trip, our income dropped by half! Sometimes God tests to see whether or not our motives are right—if we go expecting results or if our heart's motive is obedience. God will continually purify us. If you've heard a "No" from Him, then say, "OK, God. I trust You. You must have something else in mind."

The issue is not whether we get results but whether we obey the Lord in what He requires of us. We must not try to limit God in one way or another, but must simply act upon His Word. This keeps a dynamic in your relationship with the Lord. It keeps your faith up to date as well.

Robert and Pam Evans' Story

Author's Note: Another missionary couple, Bob and Pam Evans, describe a loving and interdependent relationship with their home church fellowship. It provides an inspiring model for us.

Pam: Regarding our supporters, friends, and home church, we felt like we were cutting off our arm when we left. We were breaking away from the body. So, when Bob went home, it was to patch that up and renew that deep support and flow of relationship.

Bob: I spoke at church on relationships—the body of Christ ministering behind you. If you don't include them, you're cutting them off from your ministry. We're working on this whole relationship principle. It's building relationship with Christ and relationship with the body of Christ that must happen before you go through the gates of missions.

Pam: If we sometimes feel we're out here by ourselves, it's due to the breakdown of relationships.

Bob: In twenty-one days of visiting back home recently, building on these principles, we saw our support doubled. We started with $750 base support, plus about $150 a month from other donors. We now receive around $1,450.

We simply visited the same people we knew before. We were strengthening relationships and more. It was an intense time. I could only visit them in the evenings after their work.

They usually wanted to see what we're doing, so I brought picture boards. One suggestion was to have a photograph album, showing what we're doing, and then going back in a few years to give them an update. Then they're more enthused. to get behind us.

Our home church gives us $750 a month support, but they actually give much more than that. Every time we go on an outreach, they send us extra money, and every few months, they send us extra. They love what we're doing. Now they want to do more. They don't want us to feel like we're a burden on them, but rather an extension of them. They don't want to control our ministry, but they want to have a part in releasing our ministry. They want to be involved at the prayer level in every major decision we make. That means at the beginning of things. They said they were going to contact their other missionaries and start making this policy.

Pam: Sometimes, as a missionary, you write the church with all the facts about where you're going, what you plan on doing, and ask if they can help you financially instead of bringing them in sooner in the decision-making and prayer stages of your plans.

Bob: They really want to be part of everything. If they're sending you out, they want to know. Our church may be unusual. But I've started to see this throughout the mainland churches that are becoming more missions-minded.

I think almost any church would be drawn into more of a relationship with their missionaries if they were involved from the start, beginning with prayer.

Pam: Our friends, the "heart relationships," said, "Let us know your needs. We can't guess." I've always been shy about blurting out all our needs in a letter. What do you really share? And they came back and said, "We need to know. We want to know." That was a relief for us to be able to feel free to write, to be transparent.

Eliot Henderson's Story

Author's Note: I first met Eliot in Kona, Hawaii, when he was a single missionary-in-training on his way to the Philippines. His lifestyle of communication with his support team has been a tremendous inspiration to me and many others.

I consider myself successful [in support raising] not because of the amount of money I receive but because I never lack in resources for what God has called me to. I've never had a time when my support didn't step up to the level of my need.

For instance, when my wife and I had our first baby, the support rose before I realized the extent of the upcoming need. The Lord knew we needed the money, and made provision before I'd come under the burden of it. I'm free from debt and wanting.

The key reason is that the Lord called me to the Philippines. I knew it was His idea, and I went in obedience to Him. That is the foundation of why He's made provision for His will to be done. The call was first. I'm where the Lord called me.

In my case, the Lord met my needs without my having to write a newsletter asking for money. One special couple from Nevada started supporting me without any solicitation. I was in charge of the grounds crew at YWAM's headquarters in Hawaii, and a man named Lee worked with me for two hours a day for his student work duty. I shared with him what I was doing, and one day he said, "My wife and I have decided to support you for a year." They also shared with others back home in Nevada. As a result one guy has occasionally sent checks.

My first newsletter asked for prayer for direction. I explained I was planning to go to the Philippines. By the time I sent the second newsletter, people had come out of the woodwork to give me support, making it possible for me to go. Ever since, my support has increased to meet my needs, and later, when I married, my family's needs.

Although I don't have anything against it, I've never come out and asked for money. I believe that the newsletter is a ministry in itself to bless and encourage and share the work. I always remember how hard supporters work for the money they give. I feel obliged to give them a good accounting of what I'm doing. The Lord has honored that by providing all the support I need. I try to keep my focus on Him.

I also make it clear to supporters that my work is their work. It's our work. My part is to be out there doing it, and since the Lord has called me to this, it's never a strain or a sacrifice for me. My supporters are being faithful to do their part—to give. As a team, we get the work done together. They're fighting the battle as much as I am.

In my letters to them, I give newsworthy information, like telling about people who have been led to the Lord, a miraculous healing, someone I helped by giving money, or if I've built a house for someone. I also include the work my wife does. I try to make it real without exaggerating the truth. There is a tendency to paint an exaggerated picture short of telling blatant lies. You have to check yourself to make sure you're not manipulating people.

I never paint myself as a great professional missionary or superstar, but I let people know in my letters how frail I am and that I'm a real person. I have fewer abilities than anyone I know out there. I didn't have any talents to offer the Lord. I had been on drugs and had no skills I could put to use like some people. All I had was a willing, thankful, and loving heart because of what the Lord has done in my life. Everything else I've learned on the job.

If I did it, anybody could do it. It's important not to communicate to people, "I'm a couple of notches above you. You're just a regular working civilian."

I just communicate, as honestly as possible, what's happening in my work. I try not to use the word "ministry," for instance. I refer to it as "our work," or "my work," or "their work." I may mention "in our prison ministry," but I don't mention "ministry" in every other sentence.

I believe in tithing and do tithe. Actually, I go well in excess of that. I also give money to help sick kids, get people out of jail, and help to build houses, etc.

Sometimes when I'm generous, I feel like, "Oh, boy, I've really blown it this time. I've really pulled the rug out from under us." But the Lord has always provided for us.

I send out a hundred newsletters every two months. I can't personalize all of them the way I'd like to, so I concentrate and pour out my heart to the people who are supporting us. I write twenty long letters to people who support us, spending at least an hour writing each one, as I have to dig down deep. That's twenty long ones—twenty hours. However, time flies when I'm working on those.

I used to photocopy handwritten newsletters and then personally write on the back of each one an additional section. I've switched to typing, because it's too laborious to write clearly. Sometimes I just sign and mail it. I send about thirty-five through a friend in California who copies my letter and sends them out from there. These go to people I never hear from, but I still want to send the letter.

Sometimes I sit down and start writing and realize I'm being used by the Holy Spirit. I can feel the Spirit working to encourage and bless that person. I'm not just talking about people who give money but also others I write to. I could almost make it a full-time job!

Every two or three newsletters, I enclose a photo of me or my family or the kids at the jail. It's an investment, and people love it. When I get a newsletter, I rip it open and look to see if the sender wrote on it. If it's only signed with a name at the bottom, sometimes I don't even read it, I just file it.

You cannot invest too much in your supporters. They're blessed out of their socks when they hear some of the things we take for granted.

I used to envy the people who had a church behind them paying $500 or $1,000 a month. Now we have people who support us $50 here, $50 there, or $100 here. I've seen missionaries with church support all of a sudden receive a letter saying, "We have to cancel your support. We've fallen on hard times and are cutting back 50 percent." Those missionaries were devastated. They almost had to pack their bags. All their eggs were in one basket.

With us, if we lose one of our supporters, we're still afloat. As a matter of fact, when we lost our largest one, we were able to take it in stride. The Lord blessed us with unexpected gifts in the mail to make up the difference. I thank the Lord that we have a number of small supporters rather than one big home-run hitter of a church.

When I thank people for their support, I make it a two-pointed thank you: I thank them first for participating in the ministry that wouldn't be possible without them, and I tell them that the kingdom of God is advancing because of their investment. Then I thank them personally because of the blessings I'm enjoying—I'm growing as a Christian, I'm free from debt, my wife and kids are eating, we have clothes to wear, and I wouldn't be on the mission field if it weren't for them. We're working together shoulder to shoulder, carrying the burden.

—

Friendship is a ship
where we may search together
the same horizons;
one seeing sky,
the other water,
where they meet.

—

~ 10

NOTES ON
NEWSLETTERS

IN *HOW TO WRITE MISSIONARY LETTERS*, AUTHOR ALVERA
Mickelsen wrote, "Your letters back home may have almost as
much effect on the total missionary enterprise as the work you
are doing in your field. If they help recruit new missionaries
and multiply stalwart prayer intercessors, they can become
fully as important as the meetings you conduct, the classes
you teach, the witnessing you do." Newsletters, whether
printed or electronic, are wonderful and efficient vehicles of
communication to convey inspiration and information to a
wide, selected audience. They are not magic moneymakers.

For some missionaries and other Christian workers, creating a newsletter is their only effort toward raising and maintaining a support base. For the receiving person, it may be
informative but often impersonal and therefore uninspiring
and ineffective.

Our support partners, friends, and relatives deserve more
attention and care than a newsletter can provide. Our objectives are to express love and appreciation, keep our friends

and supporters informed of our ministry, and minister to them spiritually.

Make your first communication a personal one. If possible, handwrite a brief note to accompany each printed newsletter, and begin e-mailed newsletters with a personal note. Keep in mind that what you are establishing is a relationship of value. Give your correspondents encouragement and remind them of your prayers for them. Share with them what God is doing, and be honest about your own needs of any kind. If you have not written them in a long time, *do not* make your first letter or contact with them a financial appeal. Think of how you would feel.

Where the basis of our relationships is friendship and generosity, communication comes in more sizes and shapes than a newsletter, but the newsletter is vital. It should, therefore, be informative, inspiring, inventive, and inviting.

Creating a newsletter with our readers in mind helps us to see objectively the quality, performance, and fruit of our work, and to identify the detours and appendages that waste our time and their money. Our obligation is not to preach but to inform, encourage, develop greater friendships, edify our friends, and evoke responses of widening obedience and deepening relationship to the Lord, as we share how He meets with us in real ways and expresses His grace through our lives.

In relationships and communication, impersonal draws impersonal, personal draws personal. Our newsletter should be as personal as possible. I get many missionary prayer letters every year, some warm and friendly, others tactical and impersonal, most somewhere in between. I need to remember that all of them—even those mass produced with computerized address labels—come from dedicated people with different personalities who took the time to write the letter, have it printed, process the computer labels, and prepare the envelopes. Whether they are mailed or e-mailed, newsletters deserve my attention (if not my support), but I can't help responding with more warmth and interest to the more personal presentation. Few friends treat friends impersonally.

Everyone is barraged with mail, both snail mail and e-mail; we live in a mass communication, junk mail world. Our quiet newsletter could easily become a lost voice among many others screaming for attention. It needs to stand out from the parade and penetrate into the friend realm.

Important First Impressions

We love to hear from friends. We don't love to hear from institutions. We sort our mail accordingly. If a letter looks like it comes from a friend, I open it. If an e-mail begins with a personal note, I read it.

Some people never open the impersonal bulk mail that comes to their doors and in-boxes. Most conventional mail with less than a first-class stamp goes into the trash can.

Missionary newsletters are best sent first class. Commemorative stamps are fun. Once, first-class stamps honoring Pan America gave color and an international flavor to America's mail. Missionaries on the field who have people back home handling their newsletters can request that they use commemorative stamps. Even better is to send letters from the field periodically with foreign postage stamps. We all enjoy receiving international mail.

Whenever possible, hand write the addresses. Hand writing is much more personal than computer-generated labels. If it is necessary to save time, then use attractive return address labels.

If you are sending your newsletter as an e-mail or as an e-mail attachment, be sure to send it from an address recipients will recognize, and whenever possible begin each e-mail with a special note to that individual. If your letter includes any special formatting or photos, it is a good idea to test send it to a few friends before e-mailing it to the rest of your mailing list. Your friends can give you feedback about any compatibility problems and tell you how your letter will appear on the receiver's end. Were they able to receive and open the e-mail and/or the attachment easily? Did the letter's appearance remain as you intended it? Because what looks good on your screen may not transmit as you planned, this test run can help ensure that your newsletter will be accessible and inviting. (See chapter 6 for more on e-communication.)

Whether your newsletter is printed or electronic, be creative in your communication, both in format and type. Variety gives freshness. For printed letters, different colors and different sizes of stationery and envelopes create variety and are eye catching. Ask the Lord to inspire you with imaginative ways to communicate.

Avoid creating confusion or a poor image. If our newsletters look shoddy, people will expect our ministry to be shoddy. Our newsletter's image will influence whether others want to be a part of our ministry or not. Westerners especially will evaluate the quality of our work by our letters. If the presentation is clean and clear, they will regard the ministry as high quality.

Text

Text should have a natural tone, straight from the heart. If I concentrate on the fact that I'm writing to forty or one hundred people with different perspectives, I get weird. I'm not me. It doesn't fly. I need to tell Joe and Susan this and Frank that. I begin to sound like a press release or a salesman. So, I write to one person, somebody I'm comfortable with, someone I want to share my heart and life with. I use that letter as my newsletter. It keeps me honest and natural.

Between newsletters, jot down ideas of items or thoughts to include in your next letter. Ask the Lord for guidance as you prepare for and write your letter. Ask Him to help you include things that will bless those who read your letter. The better preparation you do, the easier and better the actual writing will be.

Don Richardson, missionary and author, teaches on "heft," conveying a vital point by using few—then even fewer—words. We can say more with less. We use short sentences with punchy, powerful words. The more we consolidate, the more impact we produce. We generally write too many words anyway, and people end up not reading our letters. When you write your first draft of a newsletter, expect to cut it down significantly. Rewriting is an important part of writing.

If possible keep your newsletter to one page. If it is two pages, use only one side of the paper. It will be more likely to be read. Have breathing space with good margins and space between paragraphs, and include photographs or drawings.

Catch your reader's attention in your first paragraph. Make it either inviting in a friendly way or dynamic in impact, perhaps with an interesting story of a recent event.

Send bits of information, not a flood. Send different types of information at different times. Build on the last letter. Include personal as well as ministry information. Make your coworkers on location real to those you write so they may pray for them too. Tell of their work and needs.

Don't preach, but share the word of your testimony. Pray that God will use it to encourage and build up your readers.

Underline or highlight important events or items for prayer.

Avoid raising unnecessary questions. An overly detailed budget can distract on little elements. A single paragraph attempting to summarize an entire week's revolutionary teaching can make your friends question your theology (it happened to me!).

On the other hand, we need to be specific about our needs. We feel bad when we find out too late that someone had been hurting in an area where we could have helped but we didn't know. Our supporters want to know what our needs are, or they would not be our supporters. Most Westerners don't like hints; they prefer specifics: what the need is ($1,500), the time frame for response (within three weeks), and the purpose for the donation (transportation to a specific field). Do we need an additional $200 a month for regular support? Could they help by sending $5 or $50 a month? Who should they send it to? (Checks payable to...; envelope enclosed.) They need an opportunity.

Look at it as if you were sowing seeds, then watch God do the selecting. What you need will come in the right time in the right way. But be careful: presenting a need like this must be "culturally tailored"—in some cultures, candor is appropriate; in others, it is offensive. Keep in mind both the recipients of your letter and its destination.

One missions professor assigned a survey of missionary prayer letters. The result was shocking. His students discovered that most of the letters had little if anything to do with prayer but were cosmic, super-spiritual expressions of God's blessing in a picture-perfect generalization, without any concrete description of what was happening in the field. Nothing tangible. Nothing to put a handle on in prayer.

Humility must be expressed through our letters. We need to be honest about our problems while blending them in with the victories, e.g., "I'm struggling with the heat and crowded conditions. The worst, however, is the bugs! But this morning during my quiet time, God showed me...and it was wonderful. Now I know how to handle this other problem." The fact that God meets us in our humanity, in our brokenness, and then redeems the situation, gives hope to others. It's also a more honest reflection of the truth.

When writing donors, one missionary tests herself with this: "Have I gone one step beyond my comfort zone? Have I shared a little bit more honestly than I'm comfortable with?"

This honesty opens doors for her donors to be more open to God's work in their own lives, to be more closely knit with her, whether through prayer support, finances, or love.

One missionary friend of mine writes incredibly vulnerable prayer letters. Each time I receive one of his letters, I think, "What shocking thing is Robby disclosing this time?" Robby intimately relates his personal struggles with his self-esteem, yet how the Lord is meeting him; how he's felt like a failure at times; how he walked into the office one night, felt like giving up, but the next morning God spoke to him. He shares how much money he gives away (usually more than he keeps). He uses a sizeable portion of his income to maintain a fleet of cars for other missionaries to use and does all the maintenance personally.

He mentions things in his newsletter that normally we might shy away from. He's transparent. He's honest. And he's living a life of generosity. People are impressed with his servanthood and ministry. It challenges them in their own lives. Also, my friend is generally amply supplied with support as people watch his life and respond. His servant attitude and vulnerability are infectious. They draw others in.

The word of our testimony is where power and inspiration lies. "They overcame him [Satan] by the blood of the Lamb and by the word of their testimony..." (Rev. 12:11). Our testimony always involves describing a frail human being in his or her weakness (King David or the apostle Peter, for instance) encountering the amazing God in strength and bringing something remarkable out of it.

Some of my supporters report that they were never interested in missions before; they supported me because they liked me, not missions. Now they tell me that because I've communicated my frailty and what God is doing not only in my life but also in the lives of others here and in the field, their vision has been expanded. Some are even entering the mission field. What an inspiration to keep deploying myself in both directions, into my ministry as well as into those whom God has planted in my life.

Proofreading

Have someone proofread your last draft to screen for typos, grammatical errors, clarity, and flow of text. If obvious errors exist, our readers will react to our lack of carefulness and wonder if we're also careless in our ministry. Pick a trusted friend who will be honestly critical of how the letter sounds. The proofreader's objective insight often prevents misunderstandings. With a proofreader's feedback, we can correct ourselves before our creation "hits the newsstands." Perhaps we worded a phrase in a way that will produce unexpected and detrimental results.

Personal Touch

A personal note, even if only a single sentence at the beginning, at the end, in the middle, or along the margins, lends a touch of excitement to each letter. It involves the recipient and recommits to the relationship. For printed letters, use a colored pen so the recipient will see immediately that it's your handwriting and your personal touch. For e-newsletters, use formatting to bring attention to your personal note, or make it immediately clear through what you write that the note is specific to the recipient. If there is no personal note, it's likely our letter will be put aside for later reading, perhaps "never reading."

Photographs

Photographs speak powerfully and capture what we are trying to communicate. A picture is worth a thousand words! Add a little caption. Captions are more likely to be read than the main body of a newsletter. Choose captions wisely to convey your most important information or thoughts.

Creating newsletters of mostly photos and captions will have more impact than any ordinary newsletter. For one of my newsletters, I reproduced a photo montage of my outreach to the Philippines. After my outreach to Thailand, I reproduced photos of distinctive Thai structures, especially the tiny houses in front of each Thai home where demons are offered residence. I wanted to portray the spiritual needs of the people. I often include my own picture on my newsletter to convey the feeling of my presence as much as possible.

Avoid picture postcards that endorse a stigmatized image such as "fun in the sun," especially from places not associated with the traditional view of what the mission field should be (Europe, North America, tropical islands, etc.). The stigma undermines the legitimacy of our ministries. People associate such places only with tourism and expensive pleasure, and they may feel that the kingdom of God could have no work or purpose in such an environment. That attitude poses a communication challenge.

We counter that communication problem by promoting our purposes for being there. For instance, when I first arrived in Hawaii at YWAM Kona's University of the Nations (formerly Pacific & Asia Christian University), I collected stamps from the office (we receive thousands of letters from all over the world). I used copies of the stamps to form a border around my newsletter to convey the international flavor of our ministry—to Asia, the Pacific islands, and many other parts of the world.

I still try to create a concrete picture of overall involvement in international ministry by all of us here. This includes those in food service who are directly connected with worldwide outreach by feeding others who, next week or next month, will be taking the gospel into all the world.

Gifts and Enclosures

Prayer cards provide a significant and meaningful reminder to your friends that their prayer support is essential for your ministry. Consider revising your prayer card every few years so that people continue to have your updated photo and contact information at their fingertips. (See sample prayer card formats in the "Helps and Forms" section.)

Other enclosures can be scraps of local color such as clippings from the local paper or a description of a local incident, something funny, touching, or even sad that has occurred in the local community; pressed flowers; a feather; a shell. None of these cost anything, but can bring a whiff of another land—your land—to your correspondents.

Little (flat) gifts from the field are fun to enclose in newsletters. I have sent Kona coffee packets in my letters and written, "Have a cup of coffee while you read my newsletter." Tea bags from different countries, brochures, bookmarks from the local people, anything that conveys the culture and the land, is appropriate. Once I included two Garfield cartoons to call attention to the fact that I was writing this book. (I had mentioned it before, but no one had remarked about it.) After I used the cartoons, one supporter responded, "Did I miss something? I'm sure you mentioned it before, but I didn't realize you were writing a book."

A creative teacher in a mission school writes her thank-you notes on her students' art work. We may find other creative items related to our ministry which could be used as stationery to write on.

Another form of gift is a Scripture verse, poem, or other quote selected especially as a blessing for our friend(s). Try sending a postcard with a brief note, like, "I was praying for you this morning. This verse came to mind for you. Hope it's a blessing to you, my friend!"

Response Cards

Encourage a response. Write personal questions in the handwritten note, inviting their notes and cards. Consider enclosing a self-addressed postcard for them to return. (If it is done diplomatically with those to whom we are close, or with humor, it will work.)

Ask for feedback from donors and others receiving your newsletter—personal news in their lives, including prayer requests. Ask them to pray for you and let you know if God speaks to them on your behalf. It's their ministry too, and they are removed just enough to listen objectively.

In some Western cultures, people find it "too hard to respond" to financial needs because we don't include appropriate response cards to slip in with the monthly bills. And they forget. This may be part of providing an opportunity rather than experiencing, "...indeed you've been concerned, but you had no opportunity...."

Let them know if they're getting a tax benefit. It's good stewardship for them to be able to calculate their tax deductions. I include at the bottom of the letter: "Checks should be made payable to YWAM or to University of the Nations for tax-deductible purposes." I also instruct my supporters not to write my name on the support check, because that could forfeit a tax deduction claim if they do. (See "Helps and Forms" for sample forms.) Missionaries can measure the difference between mailing one month without a response card and mailing the next with one. The difference is amazing because the card makes it easy to respond. More importantly, some return the cards with their prayer requests written on the back. That makes it easy for me to remember how to bless them in prayer.

Mail History

Keep copies of your own letters for reference, and follow up on news items in subsequent letters. More important, keep letters you receive. We feel discouraged when we receive letters from others who either didn't read our last letter or forgot what it said. So do they. It's frustrating to visit folks we recently mailed a newsletter to and have them ask what we've been doing. In the same way, we don't remember every detail of their letters to us either. When I go home, I try to carry the latest letters with me so I can reread them right before I visit the people. It's warm and wonderful to have someone acknowledge something special and deep in our lives. It shows they care.

Timing

Write regularly—at least every two to three months is recommended.

Some may want a monthly list of prayer requests to keep current, but most will feel that monthly letters from you are a bit much. Send a newsletter periodically with personal postcards, notes, or letters in between to supporters and close friends or family. Even if we don't have time to write much, we can send something. Short, quick notes are excellent. Postcards are simple and very personal.

Finally...

Pray over your letters as you send them out. Pray for each person to be encouraged and edified. "Let us be concerned for one another, to help one another to show love and to do good" (Heb. 10:24, Good News).

＿

I am loved.

It is enough for now that
some few have reckoned my
faults and frailties
as chaff to my grain.
To these, I owe the same
generous sifting.
To the world at large
I owe this simple charity,
because of those dear few.

＿

– 11

FINAL
THOUGHTS

DURING THE LAST WEEK OF WRITING THIS BOOK, I revisited the cliffs overlooking the Pacific. On this occasion the winds were not violent, as they had been on my last visit. Since the winds were relatively calm, I noticed the barrenness of life at the cliff's edge: scruffy, sparse plants hung with bare roots exposed by continual erosion. The badgering of the salty air and harsh storms had taken its toll.

A grove of spindly trees overlooked a small bay. Most of the trees were dead or dying. *All* were mutilated by the elements. They were just hanging on; certainly *not* thriving. Like many missionaries without a strong support system, they were simply clinging to bare existence.

Behind the spindly trees, other trees were flourishing in that grove because they had fertile soil and extensive root systems. Their spreading growth offered an umbrella of protection from the elements. Lush ferns and grasses flourished below their canopies. Only the trees at the eroding edge were dying; those rooted deeply in fertile ground thrived. Once again, the visual display of God's master plan impressed me.

"...Not that others might be relieved while you are hard pressed, but that there might be equality. At the present time your plenty will supply what they need, so that in turn their plenty will supply what you need. Then there will be equality, as it is written: 'He who gathered much did not have too much, and he who gathered little did not have too little'" (2 Cor. 8:13–15).

Just before I finished this book, I was on a plane flying from Indianapolis to Denver. My seat was in the last row, next to a man who was reading management training material. With my background in business management, I was immediately interested and struck up a conversation.

He was a certified public accountant on his way to a management training conference. I began telling him about YWAM, our university, and the innovative projects with which we are involved. I showed him our latest international university catalog, a project which I had just finished.

As we talked, the man became more interested. At one point I mentioned, "There are seven thousand full-time staff worldwide, and none of us gets paid!" He looked at me with shock. I said, "Most of us are supported by our churches and friends and family..." He quickly responded, "Oh, I could *never* do that!" I immediately began telling him how God is faithful to provide for our needs and, "Yes, you could do it!" I honestly wanted to encourage this man in his faith.

His wife had just had their third child, and he was deeply committed to his family. I was praying for the Lord to use me to encourage him to consider involvement in missions.

However, the results was different than I expected! As we were standing up to get our carry-on luggage, he asked, "Now, tell me how this works again...what do people do? Do they send money sporadically or what?"

I answered, "Some do, but most of my support comes from monthly donors. Some give $10, several give $100, most give between $20 and $50 per month." I thought he was still perplexed by this unorthodox financial system.

His next statement shocked me: "I'd really like to be a part, but I don't think I could ever do what you're doing. I really respect it. I can give, but I don't think I can go." He then asked me how he would go about supporting my ministry.

My jaw dropped. "I've never had this happen," I said. "This is amazing! I'll have to put this in my book I told you about." God's surprises and creativity never cease to go above and beyond all that I could ask or imagine.

Over the past twenty-plus years, I have been challenged by the Lord to give of my "plenty," living a lifestyle of generosity. As I have done this, my needs are met. My plane experience was another incident of my "plenty" igniting a spark of generosity in another.

I've observed many others whom the Lord has significantly blessed. I see the same principles being honored in their lives. Even small acts of friendship sown along the way reap acts of friendship and generosity.

Generosity among believers creates interdependence, reflective of the church in the second chapter of the book of Acts. It is a privilege to be called, even "forced," into a lifestyle that nurtures interdependence with others. Raising support is one way of being gently forced into it. We are a privileged crew!

Giving and receiving does not leave the giver in poverty but rather in a balance—all needs are met. Can you imagine the difference in today's world if giving and receiving were a significant part of everyone's life? If only Christians lived a life of excellence in generosity, what a different world it would be! We would not see such rampant starvation, inequality, and brokenness.

Buying and selling is based on exact trade, but ironically, if it is our consuming lifestyle, it robs us and the world of the balance that comes through generosity. Giving and receiving makes it possible for those with "much" not to have "too much" and those with "little" not to have "too little" (2 Cor. 8:15).

Remember Paul's words to the Corinthian church: "Whoever sows sparingly will also reap sparingly, and whoever sows generously will also reap generously. Each man should give what he has decided in his heart to give, not reluctantly or under compulsion, for God loves a cheerful giver. And God is able to make all grace abound to you, so that in all things at all times, having all that you need, you will abound in every good work" (2 Cor. 9:6–8).

We can grip this passage in times of discouragement as well as be bolstered by Hudson Taylor's statement, "God's work, done in God's way, will never lack God's supplies."[1] If we're not experiencing God's supply, we are usually missing something of God's ways (unless we've missed God's will!). We will have all that we need to do every good work to which He's called us.

Throughout this book, principles of "God's way" are portrayed to show that we need never be without His supply. Remember that "the one who calls you is faithful and he will do it" (1 Thess. 5:24).

Note

1. Frank Houghton, comp., *The Fire Burns On: China Inland Mission Anthology 1865–1965* (London: Overseas Missionary Fellowship, 1965), p. 93.

May the favor
of the Lord our God
rest upon us;
establish the work of our hands
for us—
yes,
establish the work of our hands.

Ps. 90:17

STUDY QUESTIONS
(FOR PERSONAL APPLICATION OR GROUP STUDY)

Chapter 1

- Have you ever experienced (or do you now have) fear about raising support for missions? Has this fear hindered you from stepping out in obedience to God's call on your life? Ask the Lord to reveal to you your fears in this area and to show you how to overcome them.

- In this chapter, the author asserts that "the security of our calling will be frequently tested." Take time to settle this issue of calling before the Lord, making notes of how and why you know that God has called you to your ministry.

- Have you believed that it is not a virtue to depend on others for support? Do you still believe this? Why or why not?

- Are you embarrassed at the thought of having to depend on others for financial support? If yes, how has your culture conditioned you to believe this concept? Is there a biblical model for believing otherwise?

- The author says, "…the more we try to be strong without the help of others, the more we are weakened. At the same time, confessing our weaknesses and admitting our need for God and others strengthens us." Do you agree or disagree with this statement? Explain your answer.

- Explain the difference between "interdependence" and "avoidance of responsibility."

- Are you a tree with a wide network of roots, or a lone tree with shallow roots (in terms of support network)? Ask the Lord now to broaden your foundations, in preparation for the "storms" to come.

- Ask the Lord to show you your own personal conviction about support raising. Do you believe it is fundamentally a good activity, or do you secretly disdain the thought of involving others in supporting you?

- Consider the various Scripture passages cited in chapter 1 about God's ways of supporting His workers. What are some themes you see in these verses? (See Exod. 25:1–2, 35:4–5; Num. 8:14, 18:21–24; Deut. 14:27, 16:17; 1 Sam. 9:7–8; 1 Kings 17; Neh. 2:1–8, 13:14; Matt. 10:5–15; Luke 8:3, 10:1–8, 22:35–38; Acts 10:2–5, 20:32–35; Rom. 15:20–24; 1 Cor. 9:14; 2 Cor. 1:16; 2 Cor. 8–9. 12:13–19; Gal. 6:6; 1 Thess. 2:9; 2 Thess. 3:7–10; 1 Tim. 5:17–18, 6:17–19; 3 John 5–8.)

Chapter 2

- Describe differences between a fund-raising approach and a friend-raising approach for developing a solid support base.

- What are some key elements of a good friendship, and how are you incorporating them into existing relationships?

Chapter 3

- How does an attitude and practice of generosity relate to support raising?

- What does practicing generosity do in the lives of the giver and the receiver? How can our generosity release generosity in others?

Chapter 4

- Take stock of your communication record. How often do you communicate with those who pray for and support you? Are you faithful to let them know what is happening in your life and ministry? Set goals for regular communications with your support ministry team.
- Are there people you are not communicating with for fear of letting them know your needs? Ask the Lord if there are some whom you might contact to become a part of your support team.

Chapter 5

- Consider whether you have been looking to people or to God as your provider. Review some of the scriptures listed in this chapter as an encouragement in your walk of faith in regard to finances.

Chapter 6

- How can you either begin or improve on communicating with friends (whether or not they support you or will support you) in the following ways: face to face, by telephone, by e-mail, through postcards and letters, through gift giving?
- Fill out the self-evaluation form found in the "Where to Go for More Help" section. Take the time to evaluate where you are now and set some concrete goals for growth in this area of communications.

Chapter 7

- As you review this chapter, consider the major hindrances to successful support raising that are listed here. Are any of these hindrances evident in your life? What can be done to rectify the situation(s)?

- Have you had any supporters discontinue their support without informing you as to why? How did you respond? What could have been or can be done differently?

Chapter 8

- What is the difference between principles and practices, and how does this difference affect the value of this teaching in a variety of economic and cultural environments?

- Respond to the comment, "the primary source of support for any missionary should come from his or her own culture."

Chapter 9

- As you read the testimonies in this chapter, take note of principles and practices that you believe the Lord might be speaking to you about. List ways that you can apply the principles in your own life.

- Paul Hawkins says, "The issue is not whether we get results but whether we obey the Lord in what He requires of us. We must not try to limit God in one way or another, but must simply act upon His Word." Are there areas where you are failing to obey the Lord because you haven't been getting the desired results?

Chapter 10

- Make a list of five to ten practices in newsletter writing that you would like to implement. For example, how often do you plan to write? Will you address envelopes by hand, type them, or use computer labels? What are some resources you want to acquire that will give you further ideas and helps in newsletter writing/production?

WHERE TO GO FOR MORE HELP

Mail-order Stationery and Gifts

Best to You—Attractive Christian stationery and gifts through mail-order catalog. Excellent discount prices for quantity orders. Write for catalog: Best to You, P.O. Box 1300, Siloam Springs, AR 72761-1300 USA; www.besttoyou.com.

Current—Mail-order stationery at good prices. Includes Christian cards, plus a large selection of all-purpose cards, notes, and stationery. Write for catalog: Current USA Inc., 1005 East Woodman Road, Colorado Springs, CO 80920 USA; www.currentcatalog.com.

Mount Carmel—"For Missionaries Only" offers Christian music and books at discount prices by mail order. For missionaries' personal use or to send as gifts to supporters. Write for catalog: Mount Carmel, P.O. Box 331, 104 Prospect Ave., Cashmere, WA 98815 USA; www.mountcarmel.com.

Prints of Peace—"Hope Kindlers for Kingdom Builders" offers catalog of Christian art, rubber stamps, and greeting cards. Write for catalog: Prints of Peace, P.O. Box 717, Camino, CA 95709 USA; www.printsofpeace.com.

Walter Drake—Mail-order personalized address labels, stationery, mailing labels, note pads, etc. Write for catalog: Walter Drake, 4510 Edison Ave., Colorado Springs, CO 80940-0001 USA; www.wdrake.com.

Audio Resources

"Walking in Financial Freedom" by Earl Pitts—six hours of teaching on four cassette tapes or four videotapes with printed worksheets offering challenging teaching on finances. Order online from www.wealthrichesmoney.org or by mail from Earl Pitts, 26 Dyer Court, Cambridge, ON, N3C 4B8 Canada. $25 + postage and applicable taxes for audio tapes, $65 + postage and applicable taxes for video-tapes (prices given in Canadian $; prices subject to change).

"Raising Personal Support: A Biblical Approach to Fund Raising," by Scott Morton, Dawson Media, a ministry of the Navigators, P.O. Box 6000, Colorado Springs, CO 80934 USA; www.dawsonmedia.com. An excellent videotape series that has benefited many mission agencies and missionaries.

Books

The Challenge of the Disciplined Life: Christian Reflections on Money, Sex and Power. Richard J. Foster; Harper & Row Publishers, New York, USA, 1989. Deals with money, its dark and light side; also on unrighteous mammon.

Debt-Free Living: How to Get Out of Debt (And Stay Out), by Larry Burkett; Northfield Publishing, Chicago, IL, USA, 2001.

The Friendship Factor: How to Get Closer to the People You Care For, by Alan Loy McGinnis; Augsburg Fortress Publishers, Minneapolis, MN, USA, 1979.

Funding Your Ministry: Whether You're Gifted or Not, by Scott Morton; Dawson Media, Colorado Springs, CO, USA, 1999; www.dawsonmedia.com. An in-depth, biblical guide for successfully raising personal support.

Generous Living: Finding Contentment Through Giving, by Ron Blue; Zondervan, Grand Rapids, MI, USA, 1997; www.ronblue.com.

Getting Sent: A Relational Approach to Support Raising, by Pete Sommer; InterVarsity Press, Downers Grove, IL, USA, 1999; www.ivpress.com.

The Gift of Giving, by Wayne Watts; NavPress, P.O. Box 6000, Colorado Springs, CO 80934 USA (excellent book on generosity).

God's Managers: A Budget Guide and Daily Financial Record Book for Christians, by Ray and Lillian Blair; Herald Press, Scottsdale, PA 15683 USA, 1981.

Growing Givers' Hearts: Treating Fundraising as a Ministry, by Tom Jeavons and Rebekah Burch Basinger; Jossey-Bass Publishers, San Francisco, CA, USA; www.josseybass.com.

How to Manage Your Money, by Larry Burkett; Crown Financial Ministries; www.crown.org.

Master Your Money, by Ron Blue; Thomas Nelson, Nashville, TN, USA; www.ronblue.com.

Money for Ministries: Biblical Guidelines for Giving and Asking, Wesley K. Willmer, editor; Victor Books/Scripture Press, 1989. Perspectives from thirty Christian leaders on funding the evangelical enterprise.

People Raising: A Practical Guide to Raising Support, by William P. Dillon; Moody Press, Chicago, IL, USA, 1993; www.peopleraising.com.

The Reentry Team: Caring for Your Returning Missionaries, by Neal Pirolo; Emmaus Road International, 7150 Tanner Court, San Diego, CA 92111 USA, 2000; www.eri.org.

Serving as Senders: How to Care for Your Missionaries, by Neal Pirolo; Emmaus Road International, 7150 Tanner Court, San Diego, CA 92111 USA, 1991; www.eri.org.

Spiritual Warfare for Every Christian, by Dean Sherman; YWAM Publishing, P.O. Box 55787, Seattle, WA 98155 USA, 1995; www.ywampublishing.com.

Wealth and Wisdom: A Biblical Perspective on Possessions, by Jake Barnett; NavPress, P.O. Box 6000, Colorado Springs, CO 80934 USA, 1987. Excellent study of finances, emphasizing generosity.

Wealth, Riches, and Money: God's Biblical Principles of Finance, by Craig Hill and Earl Pitts. Order online from www.wealthrichesmoney.org or by mail from Earl Pitts, 26 Dyer Court, Cambridge, ON, N3C 4B8 Canada, 2001. $20 plus postage and applicable taxes (price given in Canadian dollars; price subject to change).

The WORD on Finances: Topical Scriptures and Commentary, by Larry Burkett; Christian Financial Concepts, Moody Press, Chicago, IL, USA, 1994; www.crown.org.

Your Money, Their Ministry: A Guide to Responsible Christian Giving, by Edward J. Hales and J. Alan Youngren; Wm. B. Eerdmans Publishing Co., Grand Rapids, MI USA, 1981. Includes sections on Christian fund-raising, abuses and uses.

Booklets

Manual for Missionaries on Furlough, by Marjorie A. Collins; William Carey Library, 533 Hermosa St., South Pasadena, CA 91030 USA. Includes good sections on speaking engagements, slide presentations, group meetings, missionary conferences, etc. In addition, Marjorie has published *Manual for Today's Missionary.*

How To Write Missionary Letters, by Alvera Mickelsen; Evangelical Literature Overseas/Evangelical Missions Information Service, Wheaton, IL 60189 USA.

HELPS AND FORMS

The forms on the following pages are designed to be enlarged on a copier to 140 percent to fit an 8.5-inch by 11-inch page. It may be helpful to organize them in a three-ring binder.

SELF–EVALUATION

The following evaluation is designed to clarify your own thinking and aims. Keep this in your files after discussing it with your supervisor. It is, of course, confidential.

Personal

Name _____ Age _____

Names and ages of children _____
_____

Years as a Christian _____ Years in mission work _____

What do you see as your gifts? _____
_____

How would you describe what you do in your missionary service? _____
_____

What do you see as your contribution to the overall purposes and callings of your mission agency? _____
_____
_____

What is your long-term calling in ministry (in general)?
_____
_____

Do you feel that the Lord specifically called you to do what you're doing? _____

Please explain how: through prayer? circumstances? word from the Lord? _____
_____
_____

Finances and Support

Have you followed a structured, specific plan of action for financial support? _____
_____

How do you feel the Lord has led in this? _____

_____

_____

What are you now doing about support? _____

_____

_____

Do you have support from churches/individuals? _____
Is it regular? _____ Monthly amount? _____
To whom do you now look for support? _____

_____

_____

How much do these people and your church supporters know
about you, your work, your family, and your needs? Can they
adequately tell someone else about the work in which you
are involved? _____

_____

In what way has God blessed you specifically since you
became a missionary?
Finances? _____
Other? _____
How do you keep track of gifts and your acknowledgments?

_____

_____

What is your most important short-term need? _____

_____

Have finances been a frustration to you in the past? _____
If so, can you say why? _____

_____

Have you spoken with any of the missionary staff about this?

_____

Communication

Do you have a regular newsletter? _____
How often do you send it out? _____

How do you define your agency's financial policy to your supporters? (example following) _____

_____

_____

"All missionary workers with [agency] are supported through gifts of interested individuals and churches. This makes possible a mutual participation in the spread of the gospel." This is a bit clearer and more specific than saying, "We just pray for it."

People with Whom You Can Communicate

Make a list of people, using the following categories to get started:

- Pastor
- Missions committee members
- Former job associates
- High school and college friends
- Parents and grandparents
- Siblings
- Cousins
- Aunts and uncles
- Church members
- Contacts and hosts from mission outreaches

Do you consider your letter writing and communication to family and friends an integral part of your ministry? _____
If not, why not? _____

_____

How much time do you spend on this a week? _____
Monthly? _____ Quarterly? _____
Which aspects of your work have you shared with your correspondents? _____

_____

_____

About which ministries do they most appreciate hearing?

_____

_____

About which aspects of your work, or your mission agency in general, do they not know? _____

_____

_____

Can you share the overall, big picture of your agency, as well as your personal part in it? _____
How do you think they feel about your work? _____

_____

_____

_____

_____

_____

_____

BUDGET

How can you let supporters know your needs if you don't know them yourself? The following form lists items for which you may need to budget. Every three months, be prepared to give a report of your expenditures to supporters if they ask. If appropriate, demonstrate unmet needs using charts and graphs to show the percentage of income received in relation to expenditures.

Year _____

Item	Previous	Projected	Actual
Tithe			
Offerings (including pledges to other ministries)			
Start-up ministries for others (seed-sowing money)			
Housing			
Food			
Utilities			
Electricity/Gas			
Water			
Garbage			
Phone/fax/e-mail (including to supporters)			
Total utilities			
Miscellaneous household expenses			
Clothes			
Children's schooling			
Your own education			
Taxes—local, state, federal			
Social Security and insurance			
Medical/hospitalization insurance			
Other health expenses, including dental			
Travel (ministry and to see family and supporters)			
Conferences (annual amount divided by 12)			
Auto maint. (gas, oil, repairs, insurance divided by 12)			
Other auto expenses (payment, lease, etc.)			
Newsletter costs (printing, postage, photos, art)			
Stationery and other postage			
Books, periodicals, newspaper			
Gifts			
Laundry, dry cleaning			
Hospitality			
Savings (car, special projects, etc.)			
Recreation, including vacation			
Other monthly bills			

FRIENDSHIP RECORD

Name:				Date:	
Last		First		Spouse	
Address:					
Phone:					
Home		Work		Mobile	Emergency
E-mail:					
Anniversary:		B'day:		Spouse's B'day:	
Church:			Children:		B'days:
Pastor:					
How, where, when we met:					

Year:	Support Received		Communication In		Communication Out		Gifts Received/Sent	
	Date	Amount	Type	Date	Type	Date	Type	Date
January								
February								
March								
April								
May								
June								
July								
August								
September								
October								
November								
December								
	Total:							

FRIENDSHIP RECORD (continued)

Initial Contact	Date:	Type:
Response / Action:		

Follow-up Contact	Date:	Type:
Response / Action:		

Prayer Concerns	Answers to Prayer

SUPPORT MAINTENANCE AND PRAYER LETTER STRATEGY

Year _____

Month	Type of Communi-cation*	Projected Mailing Date	Date Actually Mailed	Proposed Theme	Ideas for Art and Pictures
January					
February					
March					
April					
May					
June					
July					
August					
September					
October					
November					
December					

* Prayer letter, newsletter, e-mails, letters, postcards, phone calls, visits, gifts, tapes, books, etc.

PERSONAL COMMUNICATION RECORD

This record helps track those to whom we have communicated, as well as what we have communicated. Include letters, e-mails, cards, and tapes that you have sent each member of your support group, as well as visits and phone calls.

Year _____

Name	Jan	Feb	Mar	Apr	May	June	July	Aug	Sept	Oct	Nov	Dec

SUPPORTERS' CONTRIBUTIONS RECORD

Consistent tracking is important for maintaining adequate support and healthy relationships. At a glance we see supporters' donations in order to communicate gratitude to God. We can see changes immediately and deal with them realistically. Should a supporter unexpectedly decrease or stop support, we can contact the person for clarification. **Year** _____

Name	Jan	Feb	Mar	Apr	May	June	July	Aug	Sept	Oct	Nov	Dec

PRAYER CARDS

Prayer cards give people something they can keep and use as a bookmark in their Bibles or put up as a prayer reminder. In the 1980s, I developed a prayer card that some people still have on their refrigerators! Prayer cards are important reminders to keep our lives and ministries in the hearts of those back home. Below and on the following page are several samples of format and design. Be creative, but keep your cards simple, readable, and high quality.

YWAM

*To know God
and make Him known*

Todd & Jill Smith
Kate & Benjamin

Youth With A Mission
5555 Broadway
Anycity, State 55555
emailname@email.com

serving with

YOUTH WITH A MISSION
5555 Broadway
Anycity, State 55555
emailname@email.com
www.ourwebsite.com

Luis and Ria Cruz

the
Alexanders
Steve, Debbie,
Amy, & Ian

"First, I thank my God through Jesus Christ for you all because your faith is being proclaimed throughout the whole world."
Romans 1:8

Serving in Brazil

The Ministry's Name
5555 Broadway
Anycity, State 55555
emailname@email.com

I thank my God every time I remember you. In all my prayers for all of you, I always pray with joy because of your partnership in the gospel from the first day until now, being confident of this, that he who began a good work in you will carry it on to completion until the day of Christ Jesus.
—Philippians 1:3-6

Lin Jones

c/o The Ministry's Name
P.O. Box 555
Anycity, State 55555
emailname@email.com
www.website.com

Please remember the orphans of AIDS in South Africa

RESPONSE CARDS

Printing on colored paper and enclosing a self-addressed response or remittance envelope can be very effective. Insert the appropriate names in place of the brackets.

☐ [*Missionary's name*], I want to support your ministry with [*organization's name*].

☐ I want to give $_____ in monthly support.

☐ [*Missionary's name*], I will pray for you and your ministry.

☐ Please send me prayer requests.

☐ Enclosed is a one-time gift of $_____. I believe in your work!

☐ [*Missionary's name*], please pray with me about _____

Name _____ Phone _____

Street Address or Postal Box _____

City _____ State/Province _____

Zip/Postal Code _____ Country _____

Add any special financial information at the bottom such as:

Checks should be made payable to
[*agency name*] for tax deductible purposes.

REMITTANCE/RESPONSE ENVELOPES

Many organizations provide response envelopes for their missionaries. If, however, you are in need of one, below are several suggestions for content. These can be printed by a local print shop and provide effective ways for donors and others to respond to your invitations. Use a standard #6–3/4 (U.S. size) remittance envelope, with a full flap as indicated.

Inside Top Flap:

1. Leave blank, or

2. Place your mission's corporate statement, or

3. Give instructions on how to send checks or make an Electronic Fund Transfer (EFT).

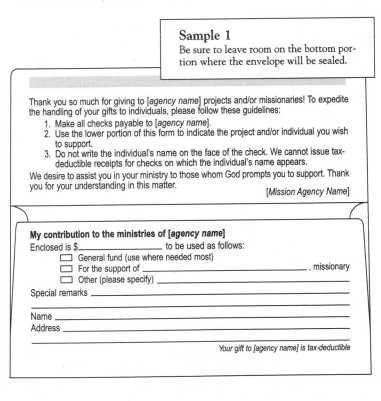

Sample 1
Be sure to leave room on the bottom portion where the envelope will be sealed.

Thank you so much for giving to [*agency name*] projects and/or missionaries! To expedite the handling of your gifts to individuals, please follow these guidelines:

1. Make all checks payable to [*agency name*].
2. Use the lower portion of this form to indicate the project and/or individual you wish to support.
3. Do not write the individual's name on the face of the check. We cannot issue tax-deductible receipts for checks on which the individual's name appears.

We desire to assist you in your ministry to those whom God prompts you to support. Thank you for your understanding in this matter.

[*Mission Agency Name*]

My contribution to the ministries of [*agency name*]

Enclosed is $_____ to be used as follows:

☐ General fund (use where needed most)
☐ For the support of _____ , missionary
☐ Other (please specify) _____

Special remarks _____

Name _____
Address _____

Your gift to [agency name] is tax-deductible

Sample 2

Either have your organization's name and accounting headquarter's address on the front of the envelope, or else put your own name and address. If you include the "Please pray with me...," your friends would probably appreciate sending those directly to you.

I would like to be a Partner-in-Ministry with _____
　　　　　☐ I would like to receive your prayer letter/newsletter/e-mail updates
　　　　　☐ I will pray for you regularly
　　　　　☐ I want to participate financially in your ministry:
One-time gift $_____ Monthly support $_____ Yearly support $_____
Please pray with me about _____
_____
Mr./Mrs./Ms. _____ E-mail _____
Address _____
City_____ State/Province_____ Zip/Post Code_____
Country_____ *Please make checks payable to [mission agency name]*

Sample 3

[*Missionary's name*], enclosed please find:
　　　　☐ A one-time gift to help with training　　$ _____
　　　　☐ A one-time gift to help wherever needed　$ _____
　　　　☐ Our regular (or new) monthly gift　　　　$ _____
　　　　☐ A note of news and encouragement
　　　　　　　　Please make checks payable to [mission agency name]
Sorry, we can't give at this time:
　　　　☐ We'll be praying for your ministry
　　　　☐ Please remove our name from the mailing list
Signed _____

Sample 4

Dear [*missionary's name*],

- ☐ Enclosed is $ _____ for your current needs
- ☐ I am increasing my monthly support to $ _____ per month
- ☐ I am unable to provide additional help at this time. I'm praying for you!

A personal note _____
_____

Mr./Mrs./Ms. _____ E-mail _____
Address _____
City_____ State/Province _____ Zip/Post Code _____
Country_____ *Please make checks payable to [mission agency name]*

INFORMATION FOR SUPPORTERS

Include an information sheet such as the one below to help prevent confusion for your supporters.

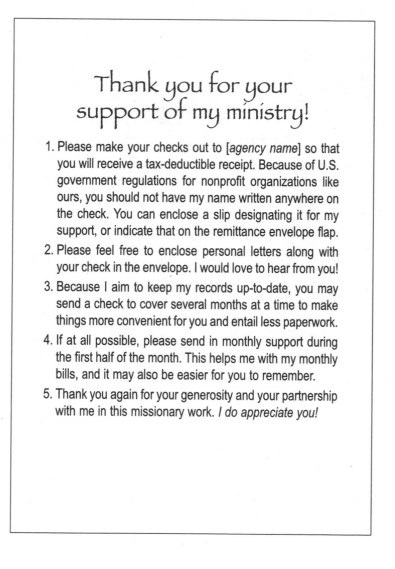

Thank you for your support of my ministry!

1. Please make your checks out to [*agency name*] so that you will receive a tax-deductible receipt. Because of U.S. government regulations for nonprofit organizations like ours, you should not have my name written anywhere on the check. You can enclose a slip designating it for my support, or indicate that on the remittance envelope flap.

2. Please feel free to enclose personal letters along with your check in the envelope. I would love to hear from you!

3. Because I aim to keep my records up-to-date, you may send a check to cover several months at a time to make things more convenient for you and entail less paperwork.

4. If at all possible, please send in monthly support during the first half of the month. This helps me with my monthly bills, and it may also be easier for you to remember.

5. Thank you again for your generosity and your partnership with me in this missionary work. *I do appreciate you!*

MINISTRY PORTFOLIO

A portfolio describing your ministry can be a useful communication tool to help your friends, family, and church better understand your work. Give a copy to key people such as your pastor, church missions leader, support team, and any other people who have a significant role in your life. Have the portfolios printed or copied on quality paper to create a professional appearance. Your portfolio could include the following items:

Cover Page—includes your name and organization, plus a logo or symbol of your organization or ministry. This page should be clean, simple, and serve as an introduction.

Ministry Statement—the next page may have a one-sentence statement to summarize ministry goals and purpose. This can be an organization motto or a statement of personal life goals and ministry purpose.

History Page—one page giving a general description of your history leading up to this point. Simply list the major events which have led to your decision to go into full-time Christian service.

Vision Page—concisely describe your God-given vision for your life—your purpose and future directions. We can boldly state what we believe God will do.

Recommendations—include recommendations from friends or Christian leaders to describe your work or organization. The portfolio's purpose is to communicate fully your organization's work and its effect in the world.

Action Photos—if appropriate, use personal pictures in a home setting and ministry times.

Goals and Objectives—list on one page your future goals and objectives. This will clearly show what it's going to take to get the job done.

Budget Page—use approximately five or six categories to list overall expenditures. Don't go into detail. Categories such as housing, food, administrative costs, office costs, transportation needs, and family expenses can be summarized, giving people a clear budget.

Financial Needs—communicate your financial status and support needs. List in exact dollar amounts how much more is needed for an adequate monthly support level.

Invitation to Respond—communicate from the heart the request to pray about becoming part of your financial support team. This should simply be a heartfelt, personal invitation which concludes with the question, "Would you pray about becoming a part of my support team?"

Response Page—include a response vehicle (such as a commitment card) that can be given to people considering becoming members of your support team.

Final Page—in large bold letters, include a statement summarizing the aim of missionary team partnership, such as, "Working together in fulfilling the Great Commission" or another appropriate phrase, perhaps one used by your mission agency in describing its ministry goals.

FRIEND RAISING VIDEO

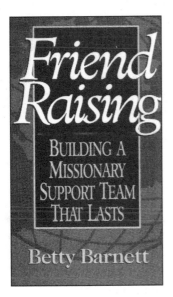

Share the Friend Raising vision with your fellow missionaries, missions students, supporters, and church!

with Betty Barnett
22 minutes
$12.00

This video is a valuable tool for full-time Christian workers in a variety of ministries and parachurch organizations as well as those preparing for or already on the mission field. Additionally, individuals and churches who want to be part of that support team will be helped to better understand their roles.

RECOMMENDED BOOKS FROM YOUTH WITH A MISSION

DARING TO LIVE ON THE EDGE
The Adventure of Faith and Finances

by Loren Cunningham, $9.99

Living by faith is not the domain of only those Christians called to "full-time" ministry. What is important is not our vocation but whether we are committed to obeying God's will in our lives. If we are willing to step out in faith, doing whatever God has asked us to do, we will see His provision. A Christian who has experienced this is spoiled for the ordinary. (ISBN 0-927545-06-3)

IS THAT REALLY YOU, GOD?
Hearing the Voice of God

by Loren Cunningham, $9.99

This practical guide to hearing God's voice shows how an ordinary man who was committed to hearing God and obeying Him became the founder of the largest interdenominational missions organization in the world. (ISBN 1-57658-244-2)

MAKING JESUS LORD
The Dynamic Power of Laying Down Your Rights

by Loren Cunningham, $9.99

We live in a world in which the protection and exaltation of individual rights has become an obsession. As Christians we believe that personal rights do hold great value. As a result, we can perform no greater act of faith and worship than to lay down these rights at the feet of the One who has gone before us, Jesus Himself! Loren Cunningham details proven steps to a transformed life of freedom, joy, and intimate fellowship with God. Includes study guide. (ISBN 1-57658-012-1)

RE-ENTRY
Making the Transition from Missions to Life at Home

by Peter Jordan, $8.99

The encouraging message of *Re-Entry* is enlightening, vital, and long overdue! Peter Jordan's insightful teaching on the challenges and opportunities that await returning missionaries makes this book essential reading for every short- and long-term outreach participant, as well as every local church and mission agency that sends out workers. (ISBN 0-927545-40-3)

WORLDWIDE PERSPECTIVES
Biblical, Historical, Strategic, and Cultural
Dimensions of God's Plan for the Nations

edited by Meg Crossman, $39.99

"*Worldwide Perspectives* is the most concise and cogent presentation of the Perspectives material that has yet been published. I highly recommend it." —**Don Richardson,** Minister-at-large, World Team

- Based on the course taken by tens of thousands of people worldwide
- Includes contributions by 50 key Christian thinkers
- Designed for both group and individual study
- Ideal for Sunday-school classes, short-term team preparation, church-based training institutes, and interdenominational courses

Worldwide Perspectives explores the biblical, historical, strategic, and cultural dimensions of God's plan for the nations through the writings of some of the most respected authorities on missions. This fascinating in-depth study has revolutionized the lives of believers around the world, equipping them to see God's big picture, expand their vision, explore options for service, invest their lives strategically, and pray insightfully. (ISBN 1-57658-281-7, 480 pages)

PERSPECTIVES EXPOSURE
Discovering God's Heart for All Nations and Our Part in His Plan

edited by Meg Crossman, $15.99

"*Perspectives Exposure* is an outstanding and user-friendly curriculum, packed with up-to-date, well-written content with wonderful potential for building awareness and mobilizing God's people for His big agenda." —**Bob Moffitt,** Founder, Harvest

Based on the comprehensive *Worldwide Perspectives*, this briefer study looks at God's work in the world through the same dynamic perspectives as the larger edition. Designed to mobilize God's people to connect their lives to His kingdom purposes, *Perspectives Exposure* explores God's unchanging purposes and investigates how His global plan is unfolding in our generation. This thought-provoking material develops global vision in practical and world-changing ways. (ISBN 1-57658-280-9)

STEPPING OUT
A Guide to Short-term Missions

by various authors, $9.99

"Short-term mission experiences can transform typical church members into radical disciples.... At last, we have a brilliant book that tells us exactly how to make these learning/serving mission tours happen."
—Tony Campolo

This tool motivates, informs of options, shapes attitudes, and helps those preparing for short-term missions adjust to new cultures and working conditions. (ISBN 0-927545-29-2)

SPIRITUAL WARFARE FOR EVERY CHRISTIAN
How to Live in Victory and Retake the Land

by Dean Sherman, $12.99

God has called Christians to overcome the world and drive back the forces of evil and darkness at work within it. Spiritual warfare isn't just casting out demons; it's Spirit-controlled thinking and attitudes. Dean delivers a no-nonsense, both-feet-planted-on-the-ground approach to the unseen world. Includes study guide. (ISBN 0-927545-05-5)

WHY NOT WOMEN?
A Fresh Look at Scripture on Women in Missions, Ministry, and Leadership

by Loren Cunningham and David Joel Hamilton, $14.99

Millions of believers are hungry for an uncompromising look at the roles of women in missions, ministry, and leadership. This book brings light, not just more heat, to the church's crucial debate through a detailed study of women in Scripture, historical and current global perspectives, and an examination of the fruit of women in public ministry. *Why Not Women?* is a powerful revelation of what's at stake for women, men, the body of Christ, and God's kingdom. (ISBN 1-57658-183-7)

CLEARLY COMMUNICATING CHRIST
Breaking Down Barriers to Effective Communication

by Landa Cope, $8.99

Today's society requires relevant communication. Landa Cope shares how readers can break even the most difficult barriers to communicating the gospel and demonstrating the character of God in their everyday lives. (ISBN 0-927545-47-0)

DISCIPLING NATIONS
The Power of Truth to Transform Cultures, 2nd Edition
by Darrow Miller, $15.99

The power of the gospel to transform individual lives has been clearly evident throughout New Testament history. But what of the darkness and poverty that enslave entire cultures? In *Discipling Nations*, Darrow Miller builds a powerful and convincing thesis that God's truth not only breaks the spiritual bonds of sin and death but can free whole societies from deception and poverty. Excellent study of worldviews. Includes study guide. (ISBN 1-57658-248-5)

LEARNING TO LOVE PEOPLE YOU DON'T LIKE
How to Develop Love and Unity in Every Relationship
by Floyd McClung, $8.99

Does God really expect us to get along with each other? Floyd McClung offers challenging and practical answers for achieving productive, lasting relationships. Here is a firsthand account of how anyone can live in love and unity with others, both in the church and in the world. Includes study guide. (ISBN 0-927545-19-5)

FOLLOWING JESUS
Attaining the High Purposes of Discipleship
by Ross Tooley, $9.99

Following Jesus brings vision and direction to Christians who want to know God and make Him known. With straightforward teaching drawn from true stories of God's faithfulness and guidance, Ross Tooley examines how our passionate and patient God leads His present-day disciples into the dreams He has for them and for His kingdom. (ISBN 1-57658-205-1)

THE LEADERSHIP PARADOX
A Challenge to Servant Leadership in a Power Hungry World
by Denny Gunderson, $9.99

What is the key to effective leadership? The ability to organize and take charge? The ability to preach and teach? Entrepreneurial skill? A charismatic personality? According to Jesus, none of the above. This refreshingly candid book draws us to the Master's side. Through the eyes of people who experienced Jesus firsthand, we discover insights that will challenge us to re-think our leadership stereotypes. Includes study guide. (ISBN 0-927545-87-X)

INTERCESSION, THRILLING AND FULFILLING

by Joy Dawson, $12.99

This book proves that we are surrounded by opportunities to impact our world through the powerful means of intercessory prayer. *Intercession, Thrilling and Fulfilling* spells out the price of obedience but leaves us in no doubt that the rewards and fulfillment far outweigh that price. We become history shapers and closer friends of Almighty God. (ISBN 1-57658-006-7)

COURAGEOUS LEADERS
Transforming Their World

by James Halcomb, David Hamilton, and Howard Malmstadt, $15.99

Our world needs courageous leaders who will recognize the need for God-motivated action and follow through with a God-led plan. Whether your vision for change is local or global, simple or complex, for home, business, or ministry, *Courageous Leaders* will help you remain on a true course and reach the goal set before you. (ISBN 1-57658-171-3)

CHRISTIAN HEROES: THEN AND NOW
Great missionary biographies!

by Janet and Geoff Benge, $6.99 each

This popular series chronicles the exciting, challenging, and deeply touching true stories of ordinary men and women whose trust in God accomplished extraordinary exploits for His kingdom and glory. Real people—incredible, inspiring true stories for ages 10 to 100!

Gladys Aylward • ISBN 1-57658-019-9
Rowland Bingham • ISBN 1-57658-282-5
Corrie ten Boom • ISBN 1-57658-136-5
William Booth • ISBN 1-57658-258-2
William Carey • ISBN 1-57658-147-0
Amy Carmichael • ISBN 1-57658-018-0
Loren Cunningham • ISBN 1-57658-199-3
Jim Elliot • ISBN 1-57658-146-2
Jonathan Goforth • ISBN 1-57658-174-8
Betty Greene • ISBN 1-57658-152-7
Wilfred Grenfell • ISBN 1-57658-292-2
Adoniram Judson • ISBN 1-57658-161-6
Eric Liddell • ISBN 1-57658-137-3
David Livingstone • ISBN 1-57658-153-5

Lottie Moon • ISBN 1-57658-188-8
George Müller • ISBN 1-57658-145-4
Nate Saint • ISBN 1-57658-017-2
Ida Scudder • ISBN 1-57658-285-X
Mary Slessor • ISBN 1-57658-148-9
Hudson Taylor • ISBN 1-57658-016-4
Cameron Townsend • ISBN 1-57658-164-0
John Williams • ISBN 1-57658-256-6

INTERNATIONAL ADVENTURES
Amazing True Stories of Spiritual Victory and Personal Triumph
by various authors, $11.99 each

On every continent, in every nation, God is at work in and through the lives of believers. From the streets of Amsterdam to remote Pacific islands to the jungles of Ecuador and beyond, each international adventure that emerges is a dramatic episode that could be directed only by the hand of God...

Adventures in Naked Faith • ISBN 0-927545-90-X
Against All Odds • ISBN 0-927545-44-6
A Cry from the Streets • ISBN 1-57658-263-9
Dayuma: Life Under Waorani Spears • ISBN 0-927545-91-8
Imprisoned in Iran • ISBN 1-57658-180-2
Living on the Devil's Doorstep • ISBN 0-927545-45-4
Lords of the Earth • ISBN 1-57658-290-6
The Man with the Bird on His Head • ISBN 1-57658-005-9
Peace Child • ISBN 1-57658-289-2
Tomorrow You Die • ISBN 0-927545-92-6
Torches of Joy • ISBN 0-927545-43-8
Totally Surrounded • ISBN 1-57658-165-9

A CALL TO PRAYER FOR THE CHILDREN, TEENS, AND YOUNG ADULTS OF THE 10/40 WINDOW
by Beverly Pegues and Nancy Huff, $14.99

Millions of youth who live in the 10/40 Window are growing up in devastating situations with no way of escape. Most have never heard the transforming gospel of Jesus Christ. These carefully researched profiles of sixty-six nations will guide you to a new level of awareness and targeted intercession. Your prayers that can change the life of a child and the course of a nation. (ISBN 1-57658-255-8)

THE GREAT OMISSION
Fulfilling Christ's Commission Completely

by Steve Saint, $9.99

Steve Saint, son of missionary martyr Nate Saint, shares dramatic stories from his experiences with the tribe who killed his father, in this powerful call for the inclusion of indigenous believers in the Great Commission. Learn how current missions strategies have unwittingly kept millions of believers from fulfilling their roles in God's kingdom. (ISBN 1-57658-216-7)

UNVEILED AT LAST
Discover God's Hidden Message from Genesis to Revelation

by Bob Sjogren, $9.99

Read the Bible as one book with one introduction, one story, and one conclusion. Bob Sjogren unlocks the unifying theme of Scripture from Genesis to Revelation: God redeeming people from every tongue, tribe, and nation. (ISBN 0-927545-37-3)

Available from YWAM Publishing
P.O. Box 55787, Seattle, WA 98155 USA
1-800-922-2143
ywampublishing@cs.com
www.ywampublishing.com

ABOUT THE AUTHOR

Betty Barnett began full-time voluntary Christian service in 1975, dependent upon missionary support from her church and individuals. Her home is in Kailua-Kona, Hawaii, where she leads the College of Communication for Youth With A Mission's University of the Nations—Kona campus. She also serves as executive editor for *Transformations*, U of N–Kona's quarterly magazine, and leads the Authors Training School at the Kona campus. She has a bachelor's degree in social work and a master's degree in business administration.

Betty has held various positions in YWAM, including managing editor for Zondervan's *Christian Growth Study Bible*, the first missions-focused study Bible, incorporating YWAM's discipleship training curriculum (now available in Zondervan's *Starting Point Study Bible*), and general editor for Zondervan's *Living Encounters* Bible-study guide series, also based on YWAM's discipleship curriculum. While working on these discipleship Bible resources, Betty served in Harpenden, England, for seven years through YWAM's Europe, Middle East, and Africa coordinating base.

Over the years, Betty's dynamic speaking ministry has taken her throughout the world, teaching and encouraging thousands of students and missionaries about the principles found in this book.

Prior to coming to YWAM in 1985, Betty's wealth of experience included serving as business manager and corporate treasurer for Lamb's Players (a Christian performing arts company) and project manager of Frontier Fellowship/*Global Prayer Digest* at the U.S. Center for World Mission.

For information about Betty's international speaking schedule, please contact her at:

Betty Barnett
College of Communication
University of the Nations
75-5851 Kuakini Hwy.
Kailua-Kona, HI 96740 USA

YOUTH WITH A MISSION AND UNIVERSITY OF THE NATIONS

Youth With A Mission (YWAM) is an international, interdenominational Christian mission reaching out to the world with the gospel of Jesus Christ through evangelism, training, and mercy ministries. YWAM has 12,000 full-time staff working in over 800 operating locations in more than 145 nations and each year facilitates the involvement of more than 30,000 people in short-term training and projects.

YWAM's University of the Nations (U of N) fulfills its commitment to Christ's Great Commission by equipping men and women spiritually, culturally, intellectually, and professionally and inspiring them to use their God-given abilities to communicate and demonstrate the Good News in all nations. The university faculty seeks to broaden the scope of evangelism by equipping students to serve worldwide in various domains of life. With its courses offered in 91 nations and 46 languages, the U of N has an international staff and student body. The original campus is located in Kona, Hawaii.

For more information about YWAM, including short-term training and missions opportunities all over the world, visit www.ywam.org. For information about training with YWAM's university, contact the University of the Nations:

Address: University of the Nations, Registrar's Office
            75-5851 Kuakini Highway
            Kailua-Kona, HI 96740 USA
Web sites: www.ywam.org, www.uofn.edu, www.uofnkona.edu
E-mail: info@uofn.edu, admissions@uofnkona.edu
Phone: (1) 808-326-7228